The Surrender Proceedings

April 9, 1865
Appomattox Court House

Revised 2nd Edition

This series is dedicated to the State of Virginia and all of her people who lived during the War Between the States. It is the purpose of this series to preserve, as a part of our heritage, the deeds and sacrifices of these Virginians. Your support of this project is greatly appreciated.

Number 419 of 1,000

Frank P. Cauble

Frank P. Cauble

Manufactured in the United States by
H. E. Howard, Inc., Lynchburg, Virginia

Printed by H. E. Howard, Inc.

ISBN-0-930919-40-8

The Surrender Proceedings

April 9, 1865
Appomattox Court House

Revised 2nd Edition

Frank P. Cauble

CONTENTS

DEFINITION AND SCOPE OF STUDY

The scope of this study embraces a documented report on the proceedings connected with the surrender of the Army of Northern Virginia in April, 1865. Without entering into a discussion of the military situation which produced the surrender, an effort is made to produce a comprehensive survey of the surrender proceedings, covering both the disputed and non-disputed points.

Although not all the surrender negotiations took place in the immediate vicinity of Appomattox Court House, the entire correspondence between Grant and Lee has been included in order to give a complete picture of the proceedings. A small amount of other material has been included for the same reason, but the primary emphasis is on the surrender at Appomattox Court House.

There is no scarcity of material on this subject; the story is an oft-told tale. The chief problem lies in the many conflicting reports of the same events and the numerous errors which have crept into the record. A new and careful study, as well as continued study, is necessary in order to produce a trustworthy and factual report.

Since the surrender at Appomattox Court House was one of the most notable events in American history, every effort should be made to provide the American people with a sound story of what actually happened in connection with this historic event.

GRANT'S FIRST LETTER TO LEE

The negotiations between Grant and Lee for the surrender of the Army of Northern Virginia began late on the afternoon of April 7, 1865, when Grant wrote a letter to Lee suggesting that the Confederate leader should surrender his army.

The main sources seem to be in substantial agreement about the circumstances surrounding Grant's first letter, and no serious discrepancies have been noted in regard to this phase of the negotiations.

Grant gave the following account:

> I met Dr. Smith, a Virginian and an officer of the regular army, who told me that in a conversation with General Ewell, one of the prisoners and a relative of his, Ewell had said that when we got across the James River he knew their cause was lost, and it was the duty of the authorities to make the best terms they could while they still had the right to claim anything. He said, further, that for every man that was killed after this in the war somebody was responsible, and it would be but very little better than murder. He was not sure that Lee would consent to surrender his army without being able to consult with the President, but he hoped he would.
>
> I rode into Farmville on the 7th, arriving there early in the day. Sheridan and Ord were pushing through, away to the south. Meade was back toward High Bridge, and Humphreys confronted Lee as before stated. After having gone into bivouac at Prince Edward's Court House, Sheridan learned that seven trains of provisions and forage were at Appomattox, and determined to start at once and capture them; and a forced march was necessary in order to get there before Lee's army could secure them. He wrote me a note telling me this. This fact, together with the incident related the night before by Dr. Smith, gave me the idea of opening correspondence with General Lee on the subject of the surrender of his army.[1]

In the *Official Records,* Grant outlined the military situation which existed on April 7 and then said: "Feeling now that General Lee's chance of escape was utterly hopeless, I addressed him the following communication from Farmville:".[2]

John Gibbon said that Grant mentioned his intention to write Lee to both Ord and Gibbon.

> That evening General Ord and I called on General Grant at his room in the hotel, and in the course of conversation General Grant remarked, in his quiet way: "I have a great mind to summon Lee to surrender."

I suspect that he had already made up his mind to do so, and the idea struck me as peculiarly appropriate. Forced to form his line of battle on the other side of the river to resist our further pursuit, much of his artillery and transportation in our possession, Lee's chances for reaching Lynchburg with his much-reduced and half-famished army were very slim. General Grant must have had the matter already well prepared in his mind, for shortly afterward his adjutant-general (Seth Williams) was on his way to the enemy's line with the now historic note of April 7.[3]

Horace Porter added the information that Grant spoke to Wright, in addition to Ord and Gibbon, about sending some communication to Lee.[4]

Morris Schaff emphasized the parts which Wright and Sheridan played in causing Grant to make up his mind about sending a letter to Lee.

> In the course of the afternoon, Wright, while waiting for Michie's bridge to be built, told Ord and Gibbon, who had already reached Farmville and been joined by Grant, what Ewell had said to him the night before at Sailor's (sic) Creek, namely, of Lee's duty, in view of what had happened that day, to stop the shedding of any more blood. Wright repeated the same story to Grant, thus confirming what Dr. Smith had told him; then Grant talked over with these officers the propriety of sending a note to Lee suggesting the surrender.
>
> There is no record of what Wright, Gibbon, or Ord said at this interview; but knowing that Ord had tried through his old army and fellow West Point friend, Longstreet, to bring about an interview between Grant and Lee the previous winter with a view to ending the war, I have no doubt that he urged it warmly. But perhaps what decided the matter in Grant's mind was that he knew from Sheridan's position that he would soon be across Lee's way at Appomattox as at Jetersville, and that Lee would then have to surrender.[5]

The official text of Grant's first letter is in the *Official Records,* XLVI, Pt. 3, p. 619.[6]

Headquarters Armies of the United States.
April 7, 1865 - 5 P.M.

General R. E. Lee,
Commanding C. S. Army:
General: The result of the last week must convince you of the hopelessness of further resistance on the part of the Army of Northern Virginia in this struggle. I feel that it is so, and regard it as my duty to shift from myself the responsibility of any fur-

ther effusion of blood, by asking of you the surrender of that portion of the C. S. Army known as the Army of Northern Virginia.

Very respectfully, your obedient servant,
U. S. Grant,
Lieutenant-General,
Commanding Armies of the United States.

In this letter, it should be noted, Grant addressed General Lee as the Commander-in-Chief of the Confederate Armies and said that he was asking of him the surrender, without making mention of President Davis or any other Confederate authorities. Since Grant claimed that he himself would not be responsible for any further effusion of blood, he obviously meant to say that the sole responsibility of making a decision was now in the hands of General Lee.

This letter was entrusted to Grant's adjutant general, Seth Williams, who had been Lee's old friend and former adjutant at West Point.[7] Williams carried the letter through Meade's lines, and tried to present it on Mahone's front, but had considerable difficulty in getting it through to Lee.

There was evidently some anxiety on the Union side about getting Grant's letter through the lines. C. A. Whittier, A.A.G., wrote to General N. A. Miles: "It is desired to get this through the lines tonight."[8] Miles replied that he believed it would be possible to send a communication through the picket line that night.[9]

Captain H. H. Perry of Sorrel's Brigade left a detailed account of the efforts to get the letter through the Confederate lines. He said that a flag of truce was presented from the Union lines about 5 P.M., and that he attempted to answer it, but he claimed he could not do so because he was fired upon by a number of Federal sharpshooters.

> As the top of the earthworks was reached, a number of Federal sharpshooters fired at me, and two balls passed through the uniform coat I wore, and one ball wounded a Confederate soldier in the hand, who had risen up with others from behind the works, out of curiousity to see what was going to take place. That ended the truce business for that afternoon.[10]

About 9 P.M., when the moon was about to rise, a flag of truce was again presented from the Union lines and Perry again made an attempt to answer it. Passing by the bodies of Federal dead and wounded lying between the front lines, he made contact with a handsomely dressed Federal officer. "The officer spoke first, introducing himself as Gen. Seth Williams, of General Grant's staff."[11]

Perry said that Williams first offered him a drink of fine brandy, which Perry politely refused. Then Williams handed him Grant's letter and asked for it to be delivered to General Lee immediately. Perry estimated that the letter reached General Lee within twenty minutes after it passed through the Confederate lines. This would have caused it to reach Lee about 10 P.M.[12]

Although it is not within the purpose of this study to discuss the military situation which brought about the surrender of the Army of Northern Virginia, attention is called to the fact that critics of Grant and Sheridan have maintained that the war could have been ended on April 7 if Humphreys had been given proper support at Cumberland Church. J. W. DePeyster stated that the war could have been ended at Cumberland Church, "forty miles by road and forty-six hours by time, short of the quiet surrender at Appomattox Court House; yes, ended in a blaze of glory for the Army of the Potomac, which deserved such a termination to their labors and sufferings."[13]

Whether or not Grant and Sheridan delayed the surrender of Lee's army by failing to give Humphreys proper support, is, of course, a controversial question. It seems to be a case of "what would have happened if something had happened which did not happen." Endless charges and counter charges can be based on such a premise and no final decision seems possible.

LEE'S FIRST LETTER TO GRANT

Lee was at the Blanton house, near Blanton's shop in Cumberland County, about three miles from Farmville, when he was handed Grant's first letter.[14]

Longstreet stated that he was with Lee when the letter was received, and that Lee read it in silence, and then handed it to Longstreet without any comment. Longstreet said that he read it and handed it back to Lee with the comment, "Not yet."[15]

Did anyone except Lee and Longstreet read Grant's first letter or know about Lee's reply?

Freeman apparently believed that Lee tried to keep his preliminary negotiations with Grant a close secret. He said: "Lee sent this reply promptly and did not show it to Longstreet, or, so far as is recorded, to any one else, though the nature of the message from Grant was guessed if its purpose was not actually known."[16]

This statement appears to be contradicted by the account of Colonel Charles Marshall, the military secretary of General Lee. Marshall indicated that the contents of Grant's first letter were fully known to Lee's general officers. He said: "There was some difference of opinion among the general officers as to the nature of the reply to be made to General Grant's letter, some thinking it was yet possible to save the remnant of the army."[17]

There is a strong possibility that Colonel C. S. Venable was unwittingly referring to Grant's first letter when he wrote to Colonel W. H. Taylor on March 9, 1894, that Grant's letter arrived after dark.[18] As will be shown later, the evidence indicates that Grant's second letter was received *before* dark. Since the letter which Venable read was received *after* dark, and was read by General Lee with the aid of a wax taper which Venable lighted, it was evidently Grant's first letter. It is reported that Lee said nothing for a few moments when he first read this letter. Then he asked Colonel Venable, "How would you answer that?"

"I would answer no such letter," Venable replied.

"Ah, but it must be answered," Lee said.[19]

This conversation agrees with Marshall's statement that there "was some difference of opinion among the general officers as to the nature of the reply to be made to Grant's letter."

Sylvanus Cadwallader, a newspaper reporter with Grant, said that Grant and Rawlins believed that Lee prepared this letter:

> After a consultation with the Confederate corps commanders, and one or two of his ablest and confidential staff officers, Rawlins expressed the opinion very confidently that its apparent refusal to surrender his army just then, was solely to obtain the best possible terms for many of his officers, who had made themselves liable to severe punishment by the Federal government; and the natural dread Lee would have, that Gen. Grant would take the utmost advantage that circumstances permitted. Grant soon coincided with this interpretation of the note, and made his arrangements accordingly.[20]

Colonel Charles Marshall also stated that he knew about the contents of Lee's first letter to Grant. In fact, he made the statement that "under General Lee's instructions, I wrote the following answer to General Grant's letter:".[21] Since the copy of Lee's letter in the U.S. War Department is in Lee's own handwriting, it seems that Lee either copied a letter written by Marshall or Marshall copied a letter written by Lee. It is more likely that Marshall made a copy of a letter written by Lee.

While the evidence is not overwhelming, it appears that there is sufficient evidence to justify the statement that the contents of Grant's first letter and of Lee's reply were known by a number of the officers in the Confederate Army on the night of April 7.

The text of Lee's first letter to Grant was as follows:

7th Apl '65

Genl
I have recd your note of this date. Though not entertaining the opinion you express of the hopelessness of further resistance on the part of the Army of N. Va. - I reciprocate your desire to avoid the useless effusion of blood, & therefore before considering your proposition, ask the terms you will offer on condition of its surrender

Very respy your obt. Servt.
R. E. LEE
Genl.

Lt Genl. U.S. Grant
Commd Armies of the U. States[22]

It should be noted that Lee insisted that Grant state the terms of surrender which he was prepared to offer. Lee told Pendleton the next day that he was "resolved to die" rather than submit to a demand for unconditional surrender.[23]

Lee sent his first letter to Grant very promptly, and it was soon in the hands of Seth Williams, who was waiting for a reply.

There is a slight discrepancy here between Freeman and Horace Porter in regard to the amount of time it took for Lee to answer Grant's letter. Porter said: "Lee wrote the following reply within an hour after he received General Grant's letter.[24] Freeman said: "Within an hour after the flag of truce had been met, the answer had been presented on the lines to the waiting staff officer."[25]

As previously noted, H. H. Perry said that it took at least twenty minutes for the letter to reach General Lee after it had come through the Confederate lines. It would have been almost impossible for Lee's reply to have been presented within an hour after the flag of truce had been met. Horace Porter's statement seems to have to be more realistic than Freeman's in regard to this matter.

Horace Porter said that Lee's reply did not reach Grant "till after midnight",[26] but Grant's comment implies that he did not receive the letter until near daybreak on the morning of the 8th. He said: "Early on the morning of the 8th, before leaving, I received at Farmville the following:".[27] Grant used the expression "early on the morning of the 8th" to indicate the time when he received Lee's letter and also the time when the Union troops began to leave Farmville in pursuit of Lee's army. This would probably have been at daybreak.[28]

GRANT'S SECOND LETTER TO LEE

Grant stated in his *Memoirs* that he did not regard Lee's reply as "satisfactory" but that he "regarded it as deserving another letter."[29] Elsewhere Grant said that as soon as he received Lee's letter, he "immediately replied."[30] He apparently composed his letter without consulting any members of his staff.

The text of Grant's second letter is as follows:

April 8, 1865

General R. E. Lee,
Commanding C. S. Army:
General: Your note of last evening, in reply to mine of same date, asking the condition on which I will accept the surrender of the Army of Northern Virginia, is just received. In reply I would say that, peace being my great desire, there is but one condition I would insist upon, viz, that the men and officers surrendered shall be disqualified for taking up arms again against the Government of the United States until properly exchanged. I will meet you, or will designate officers to meet any officers you may name for the same purpose of arranging definitely the terms upon which the surrender of the Army of Northern Virginia will be received.

Very respectfully, your obedient servant,
U. S. GRANT,
Commanding Armies of the United States[31]

Morris Schaff commented that Grant's second letter was "direct, candid, and generous".[32]

Schaff gave this account of the delivery of Grant's second letter:

> This important communication, like the first, was put into the hands of Seth Williams for delivery. In due time that sunny-hearted man who rode through Humphreys' troops, came up with the enemy's rear-guard of cavalry, and, although he was displaying a flag, was fired on, and his orderly wounded. He had to make several approaches to the line, and at last gained the attention of an officer of some sense, who ordered his ill-trained men to desist from firing on the flag of truce. Williams, on handing him Grant's letter, asked to have it forwarded promptly to Lee, and to make it clear to his immediately superior officer that hostilities would not be suspended on account of the communication he had given him.[33]

The question to be decided here is what time Grant's second letter reached the hands of General Lee.

It is known that the letter came through the Confederate lines before noon.[34] Thomas L. Rosser stated that the time was 10 A.M.[35]

A. A. Humphreys said that Fitz Lee sent out a flag of truce around noon to ask about the contents of the "communication of this morning".

HEADQUARTERS SECOND ARMY CORPS,
April 8, 1865 - 12:30 P.M.

BREVET MAJOR-GENERAL WEBB,
Chief of Staff:

A short time ago a flag of truce approached our skirmishers, and upon sending out to meet it we met an officer of General Fitzhugh Lee's staff who asked on behalf of General F. Lee the contents of communication of this morning and whether the communication of this morning was intended to interrupt the operations of the day. He was informed that the communication was sealed, contents not known; that it was not intended to interrupt the operations of to-day, and that the officer of theirs receiving the communication was so informed. I send this chiefly to let you know that Fitzhugh Lee's cavalry is in this vicinity and he may be attacking the rear. I have ordered a strong regiment to be sent as guard to the supply train, which I understand is close up to my rear.

A. A. HUMPHREYS,
Major-General Commanding.[36]

It should be noted here that Grant sent a dispatch to E. M. Stanton, Secretary of War, on April 8, at 12 noon which said: "I feel very confident of receiving the surrender of Lee and what remains of his army to-morrow."[37]

E. P. Alexander said that Grant's letter actually reached Lee "some time in the afternoon", and added that it was "late in the afternoon of the 8th."[38]

A. A. Humphreys said that "General Lee's answer to this second letter of General Grant was received by General Humphreys at dusk".[39] Since Lee's reply reached Humphreys at dusk, Grant's letter obviously must have reached Lee in the afternoon.

On the basis of a letter written by Colonel C. S. Venable in 1894, Freeman decided to disregard the testimony of Alexander (he did not mention Humphreys) and said that "about dark" Lee received another note from Grant. He stated that General Lee read Grant's letter by the light of a wax taper in the hands of Colonel Venable.[40]

As pointed out previously, Colonel Venable must have confused Grant's first and second letter and have held the taper while Lee read

Grant's first letter. The statements of Alexander and Humphreys undoubtedly carry more weight than the letter written by Colonel Venable, whose memory could easily have been faulty after an interval of thirty years.

PENDLETON'S CONFERENCE WITH GENERAL LEE

Sometime on April 7,[41] a number of General Lee's officers met and held a conference about the serious situation which then confronted the Army of Northern Virginia. The result of the meeting was that they decided to tell General Lee that he should stop the fighting and open negotiations for a surrender. They were willing to take the blame, they declared, for asking terms of Grant, rather than letting the blame fall on General Lee. Brigadier General W. N. Pendleton, who was not present at the meeting, was to be asked to lay the matter before Lee.

Pendleton gave the following account of this incident:

> Fighting was going on, but not very severely, so that conversation was practicable. General Gordon, from Georgia, justly distinguished as among our best sub-commanders, had with me an interview, told me of discouraging intelligence from the South,[42] and of a conference which had been held between other responsible officers and himself, and announced their joint wish that, if my views agreed with theirs, I should convey to General Longstreet, as second in command, and then, if he agreed, to General Lee our united judgment that the cause had become so hopeless we thought it wrong longer to be having men killed on either side, and not right, moreover, that our beloved commander should be left to bear the entire trial of initiating the idea or terms with the enemy. My judgment not conflicting with those expressed, it seemed to me my duty to convey them to General Lee. At first General Longstreet dissented, but on second thought preferred that himself should be represented with the rest. General was lying alone, resting at the base of a large pine tree. I approached, and sat by him. To a statement of the case he quietly listened, and then courteously expressing thanks for the consideration of his subordinates in desiring to relieve him in part of existing burdens, spoke in about these words:
>
> *"I trust it has not come to that. We certainly have too many brave men to think of laying down our arms. They still fight with great spirit, whereas the enemy does not. And besides, if I were to intimate to General Grant that I would listen to terms, he would at once regard it as such an evidence of weakness that he would demand unconditional surrender; and sooner than*

> *that, I am resolved to die. Indeed, we must all determine to die at our posts."* My reply could only be an assurance that every man would no doubt cheerfully meet death with him in discharge of duty, and that we were perfectly willing that he should decide the question. He then proceeded in, as nearly as I can recall, the words:
>
> *"General, this is no new question with me. From the first I have realized the vast disparity between our resources and those of the enemy. And although there have repeatedly occurred conditions under which we ought to have won, it was to me always evident that in prompt decisive energy, sustained by the general devotion of our people, was our hope; that in a protracted struggle we could hardly overcome the immense odds against us, unless foreign powers should in some way interfere. That they would directly or indirectly assist, I long trusted, as it seemed to me clearly their interest and duty. But these things really made with me no difference. I was satisfied we had principles and rights to maintain, which we were bound to defend, even should we perish in the endeavor."* This was virtually the testimony of a dying man.[43]

Considerable controversy has arisen over some of the statements made by Pendleton in this account of his interview with General Lee.

In his *Reminiscences,* John B. Gordon denied that he was present at the conference of officers mentioned by Pendleton. He said:

> Two days before the surrender, a number of officers held a council as to what was best to be done. I was not present, but I learned through orders that three propositions were discussed:
>
> 1. To disband and allow the troops to get away as best they could, and reform at some designated point. This was abandoned because a dispersion over the country would be a dreadful infliction upon our impoverished people, and because it was most improbable that all the men would reach the rallying-point.
>
> 2. To abandon all trains, and concentrate the entire Confederate army in a compact body, and cut through Grant's lines. This proposition was in turn discarded, because without ammunition trains we could not hope to continue the struggle many days.
>
> 3. To surrender at once.
>
>   It was decided that this last course would be wisest, and these devoted officers felt that they should do all in their power to relieve General Lee by giving him their moral sup-

> port in taking the step. General Grant had not then written his first note to Lee, asking surrender.[44]

Longstreet likewise denied that he had any part in this affair. He stated that when he was approached by Pendleton that he refused to participate and reminded Pendleton that officers and soldiers who asked their commanding officers to surrender were violating the Articles of War and were supposed to be shot.[45]

Freeman accepted the denials of Longstreet and Gordon at their face value and said: "Longstreet and Gordon had not attended the conference nor did they share the opinion of those for whom Pendleton spoke."[46]

Morris Schaff took the opposite side and said that Longstreet and Gordon were simply guilty of cringing "before public opinion, abandoning and dismantling the strong works built by those royal engineers, the inward senses of Right and Duty!"[47] Schaff also pointed out that Longstreet and Gordon did not issue their denials until Pendleton and Lee were both in their graves.[48]

Outside of the statements by Pendleton, Longstreet, and Gordon, there seems to be little direct evidence on either side of the controversy. W. T. Poague, a Confederate Lieutenant Colonel of Artillery, said that he talked with "General Pendleton who told me of the interview he had just had with General Lee at the instance of a number of his generals and it accorded with the account published afterwards of that memorable interview."[49]

It is known that Pendleton made his statements in a public address delivered at Washington and Lee University on General Lee's birthday, January 19, 1873. This address was repeated a number of times in various localities and was finally published in *The Southern Magazine* in 1874.[50] The early date at which this material was published helps to establish its credibility, while the much later reminiscences of Longstreet and Gordon could easily be inaccurate because of the failing memories of the authors. The weightiest evidence, therefore, seems to be on the side of Pendleton rather than on the side of Longstreet and Gordon.

E. P. Alexander threw his weight on the side of Longstreet but it seems that he was relying more on Longstreet's acccount than on his own memory. In his early description of the events at Appomattox, written in 1873, Alexander did not even mention Pendleton's conference with Lee.[51] He apparently included it in his later work after he had read Longstreet's *From Manassas to Appomattox.*[52]

Alexander stated that Pendleton endeavored to persuade Longstreet to be the spokesman for the group of officers, and then assumed the responsibility himself when Longstreet refused. This, too, came from

Longstreet's book, but there is nothing in Pendleton's account to indicate that he ever tried to get Longstreet to approach Lee.[53]

Alexander claimed that Pendleton seemed to be embarrassed in telling about his conversation with Lee and gave the impression that he had met a decided snub.[54]

This was contradicted by Colonel W. H. Taylor, who said that Pendleton's "report of the interview with General Lee shows that the latter accepted the suggestion in the spirit in which it was offered."[55]

LEE'S SECOND LETTER TO GRANT

Grant's second letter reached Lee along the line of march, and Lee sent a reply from the roadside where the message found him, not far from the Village of Appomattox Court House.

Lee wrote the letter in his own hand and Colonel Marshall made a copy. The text of the letter follows:

> 8h Ap1 '65
>
> Genl
>
> I recd at a late hour your note of today. In mine of yesterday I did not intend to propose the surrender of the Army of N. Va. - but to ask the terms of your proposition. To be frank, I do not think the emergency has risen to call for the surrender of this Army, but as the restoration of peace should be the sole object of all, I desired to know whether your proposals would lead to that and I cannot therefore meet you with a view to surrender the Army of N. Va. - but as far as your proposal may affect the C. S. forces under my command & tend to the restoration of peace, I shall be pleased to meet you at 10 A.M. tomorrow on the old stage road to Richmond between the picket lines of the two armies.
>
> Very respy your Obt Sevt.
> R. E. LEE
> Genl.
>
> Lt. Genl U. S. Grant
> Commg Armies of the U. S.[56]

E. P. Alexander put the following, and perhaps correct, interpretation on General Lee's insistence that he wanted to discuss "the restoration of peace" rather than just the surrender of the Army of Northern Virginia.

> Lee had but recently been appointed commander-in-chief of all the Confederate armies, and he now delays the surrender of his own army in order that the negotiation may include that of all the Confederate forces under his command. In accomplishing

> this he might reasonably hope to secure the best possible terms, as it would bring instant peace everywhere.[57]

It seems that Lee was here trying to revive a plan which he had tried once before. Lee wrote Grant on March 2 proposing a meeting of the military to discuss means of ending the war but Grant was forbidden to meet him by the Federal authorities.[58] Lee evidently hoped that Grant would now take things into his own hands and go ahead with a meeting in which the surrender of all the Confederate armies would be discussed. However, he was again to receive the reply that Grant had "no authority to treat on the subject of peace."[59]

A. A. Humphreys gave this description of the transmittal of Lee's second letter through the Union lines:

> General Lee's answer to this second letter of General Grant was received by General Humphreys at dusk, when he had halted for two or three hours to rest his troops some two miles beyond New Store, after a march of twenty miles.
>
> General Humphreys at once sent the reply of General Lee by his Adjutant-General, Colonel Whittier, to General Grant, who received it about midnight, he and General Meade having halted for the night at Curdsville, about ten miles back.[60]

THE LAST COUNCIL OF WAR

On the evening of April 8, General Lee summoned his corps commanders to his headquarters for a council of war, the last council of war ever held by the Army of Northern Virginia.[61]

Those present were Longstreet, Gordon, and Fitz Lee. Gordon was mistaken in thinking that Pendleton was in the little group.[62]

Fitz Lee said:

> The condition of our situation was explained by the commanding general to us as the commanders of his three corps, and the correspondence between General Grant and himself, as far as it had then progressed, was laid before us.[63]

It was decided that Gordon's infantry, supported by Fitz Lee's cavalry and Long's artillery, would attempt to brush aside the Union cavalry and open a way for the retreating Confederates to proceed by way of Campbell Court House and Pittsylvania. Longstreet would close up and be ready to repel any attack on the Confederate rear. However, in case it was discovered that the Union cavalry was "supported by heavy bodies of infantry the commanding general should be at once notified, in order that a flag of truce should be sent to accede to the only alternative left us."[64]

Fitz Lee said that he made an arrangement with Gordon that "if a surrender was compelled the next day, I would try to extricate the cavalry, provided it could be done without compromising the action of the commanding general, but that I would not avail myself of a cessation of hostilities pending the existence of a flag of truce."[65]

In their accounts of the last council of war, neither Gordon nor Fitz Lee mentioned that there was any disagreement at the council in regard to the attack on the morning of April 9.

This perhaps led Freeman to decide that there was complete agreement among Lee and his generals at the council of war. In regard to the decision of the council, he said: "From this decision, reached without heroics, there was no dissent."[66]

Was Freeman correct, or was there some disagreement at the council of war? Did anyone feel that an attack would be futile and that Lee should surrender his army without making an attempt to break through the Union lines?

There are several indications that there was some dissent at the final council of war.

A newspaper report at the time of the surrender quoted Gordon as saying that he had been in disagreement with Lee about making the attack on the morning of April 9.

> General Gordon informed our officers that he had not agreed with Lee in his opinion, and that from the first he was satisfied that Ord was in their front. His view, however, was overruled, and Lee made his attack this morning on the cavalry only to find behind their retreating ranks a line of bristling bayonets impossible to break.[67]

The same sort of picture was painted by E. O. C. Ord in his report of the Appomattox Campaign. Ord stated:

> General Lee would not believe General Gordon when the latter told him Ord's army was in his front, so General Gordon told me after the surrender.[68]

Weight is added to these statements by the report of Thomas L. Rosser, a Confederate cavalry officer. Rosser said:

> I reached Appomattox Court House late at night and found Generals Roberts and Gary with their brigades in position on the western edge of the village. I took position on their right, sent out scouts to watch the roads toward Lynchburg and to ascertain what the enemy was doing. Then I went to the house of my old friend, Major McLean, and spent the night in talking over our war experiences. It was upon McLean's farm that the

first battle of Bull Run had been fought and now he was about to furnish the stage whereon the last scene of the drama was to be exhibited. About 2 o'clock on the morning of the 9th Generals Gordon and Fitz Lee arrived, and, being directed to my headquarters by a sentinel in front of McLean's house, they rapped at the door, and, being admitted by Lieutenant Winston, of my staff, they came into the parlor where I sat.

NEWS.

I saw by the dim light of several tallow candles, which were burning in the room, that something terrible had happened and I at once demanded the news. "*To-morrow, morning, General R. E. Lee desired us to say to you, he will either surrender the Army of Northern Virginia or disperse it.*" I rose at once and informed these gentlemen that General Lee would not surrender me in the morning. My scouts had informed me that the Lynchburg road was clear and I began making arrangements to move off before daylight, when General Gordon assured me that if I would wait till daylight that he would go with me, and with this understanding I got everything ready and waited.[69]

Rosser was a controversial figure after the Civil War and engaged in a great deal of acrimonious debate about various phases of the struggle. If his account is accepted as it stands, it simply means that Gordon and Fitz Lee had virtually decided not to make an attack on the morning of April 9. The statement which they are reported to have made as coming from General Lee cannot be regarded as a statement authorized by the commanding general. If Rosser told the truth, it seems that Gordon and Fitz Lee were trying to nullify the decision which was made at the council of war.

It is known that Gordon and Fitz Lee held a lengthy discussion on the morning of April 9 about which one should start the attack. Gordon maintained that the enemy troops were cavalry and that Lee should attack, while Fitz Lee claimed they were infantry and Gordon should attack. Bryan Grimes said that he became so impatient at the long delay that he offered to lead the attack if Gordon would give him proper support. Grimes said that Gordon then gave him permission to take the other divisions of the corps and also left it up to him to plan how the attack should be made.[70]

Gordon did not mention any of these things in his Reminiscences. Instead of giving any credit to Grimes, he said: "I take especial pride in recording the fact that this last charge of the war was made by the footsore and starving men of my command with a spirit worthy of the best days of Lee's army."[71]

The evidence on this point indicates that the feeling in regard to the attack on April 9 was by no means unanimous. Lee and Longstreet apparently favored the attack, while Gordon and Fitz Lee evidently regarded the situation as hopeless.

GRANT'S THIRD LETTER TO LEE

For some reason, now unknown, it took the Union courier from dusk until midnight to travel the ten miles to Grant's headquarters, where he delivered Lee's second letter.

The courier found Grant at the Clifton House, suffering from a terrible headache, which various remedies had failed to relieve. Grant was upstairs with Brigadier General John A. Rawlins, both of them sharing the same bed. Others in the house heard Rawlins read Lee's letter in such a loud tone that they were able to catch most of it. Rawlins was very much displeased by Lee's letter and said that it was "a positive insult; and an attempt to change the whole terms of the correspondence."[72]

Grant took the attitude that "Lee was only trying to be let down easily" and that he could meet him and settle the whole thing in an hour.

The argument between Grant and Rawlins went on for some little time, with Grant continuing to insist that Lee would surrender, while Rawlins thought that Lee should have stated his willingness to surrender in his letter. Finally, Rawlins said that Grant had been previously forbidden by the Federal authorities to treat with Lee on the subject of peace and that Grant did not have the right to participate in the sort of meeting which Lee suggested. Rawlins was able to carry his point, and Grant's reply contained the statement that he had no authority to treat on the subject of peace.[73]

Grant's reply was as follows:

Headquarters Armies of the United States
April 9, 1865.

General R. E. Lee,
Commanding C. S. Armies:

General: Your note of yesterday is received. As I have no authority to treat on the subject of peace the meeting proposed for 10 A.M. today could lead to no good. I will state, however, General, that I am equally anxious for peace with yourself, and the whole North entertain the same feeling. The terms upon which peace can be had are well understood. By the South laying down their arms they will hasten that most desirable event, save thousands of human lives, and hundreds of millions of property not yet destroyed. Sincerely hoping that all our difficulties may be settled without the loss of another life, I subscribe myself,

Very respectfully, your obedient servant,
U. S. GRANT,
Lieutenant-General U. S. Army.[74]

At the same time, Grant also sent E. M. Stanton, the Secretary of War, copies of his correspondence with Lee, including a copy of the above letter.[75]

Grant said that he sent this letter to Lee "early on the morning of the 9th", the expression he generally used to indicate daybreak.[76]

GRANT'S RIDE TO SHERIDAN'S FRONT

Grant had breakfast at Meade's headquarters early on the morning of April 9. As soon as it was light enough, he started to ride around the left flank of the Confederate army to join Sheridan, who had been reported across Lee's front near Appomattox Court House. [77]

Grant's decision to make his way to the Union front through Sheridan's lines, instead of taking the shorter route through Meade's lines, has been severely criticized by the partisans of Meade, Humphreys, and Wright. Carswell McClellan, a Brevet Lieutenant-colonel, U. S. Volunteers, wrote two books in which he condemned Grant's action.[78] He interpreted Grant's action as an attempt to glorify himself and Sheridan and to take away the honor which rightfully belonged to Meade.

Isaac R. Pennypacker largely repeated these charges in 1933 and said that Lee's "surrender delayed some hours by Grant's riding over a circuitous route away from Meade and the vicinity of Lee and his troops to Sheridan's front, took place in Sheridan's presence and in Meade's absence as it is apparent Grant intended." He also alleged that certain dispatches from other commands disappeared, while those from Sheridan were broadcast over the North and led people to believe that Sheridan was chiefly responsible for bringing about Lee's surrender.[79]

The Meade-Sheridan controversy was in the air at the time of the surrender at Appomattox Court House. Colonel Theodore Lyman, a member of Meade's staff, expressed himself about it in a rather vehement fashion on April 17, 1865.

> How wicked are we in this world: - Now, when I should be overflowing with joy and thankfulness at these great results, I keep finding myself boiling and fuming over the personal neglect of General Meade and the totally undeserved prominence given to Sheridan. Yet Meade is really of no more consequence in this vast question of all time, than a sailor, who

> pulls a good oar, compared with the Atlantic Ocean. The truth will stand out in sober history, even for him - in the future Motleys and Prescotts.[80]

A. A. Humphreys was quite restrained in his comment about Grant's behaviour on the morning of April 9. He merely said: "Had General Grant remained on the route of the Second and Sixth Corps, the surrender would have taken place before mid-day."[81]

It will be remembered that Lee had asked Grant to meet him at 10:00 A.M., along the Richmond-Lynchburg Stage Road, between the picket lines of the two armies. In view of this request, Grant's comments on his decision to ride around to Sheridan's front seem rather strange. He said:

> I proceeded at an early hour in the morning, still suffering with the headache, to get to the head of the column. I was not more than two or three miles from Appomattox Court House at the time, but to go direct I would have to pass through Lee's army, or a portion of it. I had therefore to move south in order to get upon a road coming up from another direction.[82]

Robert S. Henry believed that Grant's action was the result of a misunderstanding and that Grant rode to Sheridan's front because he thought he was expected to meet Lee there.[83]

Lee's letter asking for a meeting with Grant was very definite, both as to time and place, and it does not seem that Grant could have possibly misunderstood it.

Sheridan explained Grant's decision by saying that Grant started for Sheridan's front because of the dispatches which he received from Sheridan after the captures at Appomattox Station. Sheridan had said: "If General Gibbon and the Fifth Corps can get up to-night, we will perhaps finish the job in the morning. I do not think Lee means to surrender until compelled to do so."[84]

Sheridan might have intended to give Grant the idea that his presence was urgently needed on Sheridan's front but it does not seem that Grant had any real doubts about Lee's willingness to surrender. He had informed Stanton at noon on April 8 that he felt very confident of receiving the surrender of Lee and his army on the next day.[85] He also told Rawlins, in the early hours of April 9, that he could meet with Lee and settle the whole thing within an hour.[86]

In view of these statements, it does not seem possible that Grant could have thought that the military situation was very urgent on Sheridan's front. Later on, Grant tried to make it appear that he was somewhat surprised because Lee surrendered as soon as he did. He said: "When I had left camp that morning I had not expected so soon the result that was then taking place, and consequently was in rough garb."[87] In such cases, it seems that contemporary statements are generally closer to the truth than the statements in reminiscences and personal memoirs, written many years later.

E. P. Alexander interpreted Grant's decision in another manner. He said that since Lee proposed a meeting to discuss peace instead of a surrender, Grant "apparently decided to make the proposed meeting impossible by at once leaving that road and riding across to the road being travelled by Ord and Sheridan." Alexander said that Grant "doubtless had an early interview in his mind when he sent his second letter, and was probably accompanying the 2nd corps, that he might be conveniently near."[88]

Alexander put a very charitable construction on Grant's decision. Needless to say, his interpretation would not be accepted by the critics of Grant and Sheridan.

It seems impossible to determine what Grant's exact motives might have been. It is known that Grant did go to Sheridan's front; that neither Meade, Humphreys nor Wright was present at the surrender conference; and that the II and VI Corps did not have any share in the surrender parade.

CONFEDERATE CONFERENCES ON THE MORNING OF APRIL 9

One of the famous sentences connected with the surrender at Appomattox Court House is the statement of Major General J. B. Gordon: "Tell General Lee I have fought my corps to a frazzle, and I fear I can do nothing unless I am heavily supported by Longstreet's corps."[89]

Gordon made this statement to Colonel C. S. Venable, who relayed it to General Lee. When the Confederate commander heard it, he is said to have remarked: "There is nothing left me but to go and see General Grant, and I had rather die a thousand deaths."[90]

The point in doubt here is when Gordon made his statement to Venable. Freeman says that it was "perhaps 8 o'clock" when Lee sent Colonel Venable forward to study the situation and ask Gordon what might be expected.[91] Although he does not state any definite time, Schaff likewise indicates that Venable was sent forward when the Confederate advance had come to a halt.[32] This seems to be the generally accepted version.

Gordon himself quoted Venable's complete statement: "At three o'clock on the morning of that fatal day, General Lee rode forward, still hoping that we might break through the countless hordes of the enemy who hemmed us in. Halting a short distance in rear of our vanguard, he sent me on to General Gordon to ask him if he could cut through the enemy. I found General Gordon and General Fitz Lee on their front line in the light of the morning, arranging an attack. Gordon's reply to the message (I give the expressive phrase of the Georgian) was this: 'Tell General Lee I have fought my corps to a frazzle, and I fear I can do nothing unless I am heavily supported by Longstreet's corps'."[93]

Here Venable very definitely said that Gordon made his statement before the Confederate attack was started. His account is so clear that only one interpretation seems possible.

Although Gordon did not actually deny that he made his famous remark to Venable soon after 3 A.M. on the morning of April 9, he did introduce Venable's report in such a way as to make it appear that he (Gordon) made his statement near the end of the battle rather than at the beginning. He also gave another version of his statement which included the words "unless Longstreet can unite in my movement, or prevent those forces from coming upon my rear, I cannot long go forward."[94] Gordon's statement quoted by Venable sounds as if it was made before the battle started. Gordon's revised statement was appropriate only for the closing phases of the battle.

It does not seem possible to reconcile Gordon's account with Venable's version of this affair. In the light of the available evidence, it appears that Gordon must have made his famous statement before the Battle of Appomattox Court House actually started, and later tried to make it appear otherwise.

While it may be of doubtful value in regard to this controversial point, it should be noted that Jefferson Davis accepted Venable's version of this matter. Davis said:

> On the next morning, before daylight, Lee sent Colonel Venable, one of his staff, to Gordon, commanding the advance, to learn his opinion as to the chances of a successful attack, to which Gordon replied, "My old corps is reduced to a frazzle, and, unless I am supported by Longstreet heavily, I do not think we can do anything more." When Colonel Venable returned with his answer to General Lee, he said, "Then there is nothing left me but to go and see General Grant."[95]

A. A. Humphreys quoted this passage from Davis and pointed out in a foot-note that "Colonel Venable stated substantially the same thing at the Lee Memorial meeting in Richmond, on the 3rd of November, 1870."[96]

Curiously enough, Freeman did not comment on this discrepancy between Venable and Gordon. He summarized the accounts in Gordon's *Reminiscences,* and in his manuscript report, and said that this was "the situation explained to Venable." But he then quoted Venable's statement of what Gordon said and relegated Gordon's version to a foot-note.[97] He did not mention Venable's statement that he received Gordon's report at 3

A.M., while Gordon and Fitz Lee were making arrangements for their attack. It seems incredible that Freeman did not note this discrepancy.

One of the peculiar weaknesses of D. S. Freeman was his inability to estimate how much time it took events to transpire. It was literally impossible to crowd all the discussions listed by Freeman into the space of thirty minutes.

According to Freeman, Colonel C. S. Venable was sent forward to talk to Gordon at about 8 A. M. Venable interviewed Gordon and returned with his report, which Lee discussed with some of his officers. After a little, he sent for Longstreet and reviewed the situation with him. Then Lee answered a number of questions which were asked by Mahone. He called to Alexander, and engaged in a lengthy conversation with Longstreet's chief of artillery. His next interview was with Colonel W. H. Taylor. Following all this, Freeman said that it was "at 8:30 or about that time" when Lee mounted Traveller to seek an interview with Grant.[98]

At least six interviews, which required five pages of text to describe, could not possibly have been held within half an hour. They must have been scattered over a much longer period of time, just as some of the individuals involved stated that they were.

Perhaps Freeman merely followed the order of events listed by Schaff in *The Sunset of the Confederacy.*[99] With the exception of Lee's interview with Colonel W. H. Taylor, the two accounts are virtually the same.

In Freeman's account, General Lee had a lengthy conversation, sometime between 8 and 8:30 A.M., with E. P. Alexander.[100]

There are at least two objectives to this time schedule. The first is that Lee would not have had time to carry on a lengthy conversation, and also conduct a number of other interviews, between 8 and 8:30. The second difficulty is that Alexander himself said that his conversation with Lee took place about sunrise.

> Soon after sunrise, on the morning of the 9th, I came up with General Lee, halted, with his staff, by the roadside, a mile and a half from the village.[101]
>
> At another place Alexander said:
>
> On Sunday the 9th we were up at dawn and soon after sunrise, after having travelled already some two miles, we came upon Gen. Lee halted at the road side at the top of a rise, the road there having woods on the left and open ground on the right.[102]

It is clear that Alexander left no doubt in regard to the time when he talked with General Lee. The place was the top of the rise, about a mile and a half from the village, and not in the rear of Gordon's command, as Freeman seemed to imply.[103]

Freeman made another error in regard to the beginning of Lee's conversation with Alexander. He said:

> Lee called to him, walked over to a felled oak, peeled off the bark, sat down . . .[104]

It seems strange that Freeman would have thought that Lee took time to peel the bark from a felled oak when he was faced with the impending surrender of the Army of Northern Virginia. He was probably led to make this error by a misprint in the published edition of Alexander's *Military Memoirs.* The text in Alexander's book reads "peeled off its bark" when it should obviously be "peeled of its bark."[105]

Alexander gave a very clear statement of what happened in the manuscript copy of his *Military Memoirs:*

> As I came up he called to me, and walking off to a clean oak log from which the bark had been recently stripped, he sat down . . .[106]

Alexander wrote several accounts of his conversation with General Lee on the morning of April 9. In an article in 1873 he summarized the words of Lee and did not put them in quotation marks.[107] Nearly thirty years later, he expanded his account quite a bit and put quotation marks around the statements of General Lee.[108] His quotations should not be regarded as exact.

Alexander said that he pleaded with General Lee to order his army to disperse rather than surrender it to Grant. Lee listened patiently to his arguments but turned the proposal down. Alexander quoted Lee as follows:

> "I can tell you for your comfort that Grant will not demand an 'unconditional surrender'. He will give us honorable and liberal terms, simply requiring us not to take up arms again until exchanged." He then went on to tell me that he was in correspondence with Grant, and expected to meet him in our rear at 10 A.M., when he would accept the terms that had been indicated.[109]

Before his conversation with Lee, Alexander said that he had decided to "take to the bushes on the first sign of a flag of truce", and that many other officers and men had similar intentions, but they decided to change their minds and stick it out when they understood it was General Lee's intention to surrender his army.[110]

Sometime before Lee started out for the rear of his lines in an effort to contact Grant, he is said to have talked with Longstreet and Mahone, both of whom agreed that surrender was the only course to be pursued.[111]

Shortly before 8:30, Lee spoke to Colonel W. H. Taylor and told him that the time for capitulation had come. He asked Taylor to accompany him during his expected interview with Grant along the Richmond-Lynchburg Stage Road.[112]

LEE'S THIRD AND FOURTH LETTERS TO GRANT

About 8:30 A. M.,[113] on the morning of April 9, General Lee rode out toward New Hope Church, along the old Richmond-Lynchburg Stage Road, in company with Colonel W. H. Taylor, Colonel Charles Marshall, and Sargeant G. W. Tucker.[114]

The Confederates rode through the lines of Longstreet's corps and sent Tucker forward with a white flag. It was the first time during the war that Lee ever appeared for any purpose under a flag of truce.

Instead of meeting Grant, as Lee had expected, they were met by Lieutenant Colonel Charles A. Whittier, a member of the staff of Major General A. A. Humphreys, commander of the II Union Army Corps. Colonel Marshall disarmed himself, took off his sword, and walked forward to meet Whittier, who brought a letter from Grant to Lee.[115] Marshall walked back about one hundred yards to where Lee was and read Grant's letter to him.

Humphreys said that Marshall "conducted him (Whittier) to General Lee, to whom Grant's letter was delivered."[116] There is little evidence, however, that Whittier had any direct contact with General Lee.

Whittier had said that he would wait for Lee's reply, if the general wished to send an answer.

Marshall said that Lee was ready to send his answer after "a few moments' reflection" and said: "Well, write a letter to General Grant and ask him to meet me to deal with the question of the surrender of my army, in reply to the letter he wrote me at Farmville."[117] This indicates that Lee allowed Marshall to formulate the exact wording of the letter and did not dictate it word for word.

The letter was as follows:

April 9, 1865

Lieut. Gen. U. S. Grant,
Commanding U. S. Armies.
General:

I received your note of this morning on the picket-line, whither I had come to meet you and ascertain definitely what terms were embraced in your proposal of yesterday with reference to the surrender of this army. I now request an interview in accordance with the offer contained in your letter of yesterday for that purpose.

Very respectfully, your obedient servant,

R. E. LEE,

General[118]

The account given here is largely based on Marshall's narrative. Freeman's account has a number of different details. Freeman said that when Marshall received Grant's letter from Whittier he "jogged back", apparently indicating that Marshall was on horseback. Marshall said that he walked back and forth between Lee and Whittier. Freeman said that Marshall handed the letter to Lee, who opened it and read it. Marshall said that he read the letter to Lee. Freeman said that Lee "dictated" his reply to Marshall but Marshall said that Lee outlined the sort of letter he had in mind and let his secretary formulate the exact wording.[119]

Freeman was evidently relying on Alexander and Humphreys for this part of his narrative. Since Marshall's account is first-hand, it has been given precedence over other accounts in this study.

Both Humphreys and Alexander have some details not mentioned by Marshall. Humphreys said that when Marshall brought Lee's letter to Whittier he told Whittier that Lee wanted to express his regret to Grant because he had not been able to see him.[120]

Alexander said that while Lee was in the rear of Longstreet's corps, Fitzhugh Lee thought that he had found an opening through which the army might escape. He gave this information to Longstreet, who sent Colonel John C. Haskell to carry it to General R. E. Lee. Haskell, astride a beautiful mare, rode at top speed to find General Lee. It is said that when General Lee saw Haskell ride up that he seemed almost more concerned about the condition of Haskell's mare than he was about the news which Haskell had brought. Lee's subordinates were probably deeply impressed by Lee's concern for a horse at the very moment when he was sending a message to Grant saying that he was ready to surrender his army. Lee evidently did not think that his nephew's suggestion had very much merit. He is said to have told Haskell to tell Longstreet to exercise his own judgment as to what he should do. It was not long until another messenger came with the report that Fitzhugh Lee had been mistaken.[121]

Humphreys said that Lee sent his reply to Grant about 9:00 in the morning and that it was placed in the hands of Meade about 10:00.[122]

When Marshall first delivered Lee's letter to Whittier, he told the Union officer that the letter required a suspension of hostilities, but Whittier said that he did not think his commanding officer (Humphreys) had any power to suspend hostilities. Marshall suggested that the commanding officer be allowed to read the letter and that he would then probably feel justified in taking the authority to suspend hostilities. Whittier came back in about five minutes with the news that his commanding officer did not think he had authority to suspend hostilities and that Grant could not be reached in time to issue an order. Marshall again requested that the commanding officer be urged to read Lee's letter to Grant, so that he could see that an attack would only mean the useless sacrifice of life.[123]

In the meantime, Lee remembered that he had failed to notify Gordon that he intended to ask for a suspension of hostilities and had not authorized Gordon or Longstreet to send out a flag of truce, pending the surrender. The proper message was evidently sent to Longstreet by the courier who had brought the report that Fitz Lee was mistaken about a road of escape being open to the army.[124]

Without any orders to suspend hostilities, the Union skirmishers began to advance and the situation looked very menacing for a while. A union courier came forward under a flag of truce and told General Lee that he must withdraw.

Finally, after Lee had again been warned that an attack was imminent, he withdrew for some distance back toward New Hope Church. About this time, word had reached Meade, who was sick and lying in his ambulance, that a dangerous situation was developing at the front, and he had authorized a truce for an hour. He sent this information by Whittier, who gave it to Marshall at what Marshall thought was sometime "after 10 o'clock."[125]

Marshall indicated that Whittier brought only a verbal message from Meade. Marshall said: "I told him I was glad to hear it."[126]

Freeman believed that Whittier brought "a note from Meade, the text of which, unfortunately, has been lost."[127]

The idea that Meade sent a letter to Lee at this time is based on a statement which Meade made in a letter to Grant at 10:00 A.M. on April 9. He said that he had written to Lee and that he was sending Grant a copy of his note.[128]

It should be pointed out, however, that Meade did not mention in his official report that he wrote any letter to Lee on the morning of April 9.[129] Perhaps he merely intended to write a letter and sent a verbal message instead.

As already stated, Marshall indicated that Whittier did not bring a written message. In his letter to Grant, General Lee simply said that "Meade informs me" and did not say that Meade had written him. In most of his letters, Lee generally made some definite references to any written communication which he received.

The Historical Society of Pennsylvania, 1300 Locust Street, Philadelphia 7, Pennsylvania, has the papers of both Meade and Humphreys. An inquiry was addressed to this Society in regard to the note which

Meade supposedly wrote to Lee on the morning of April 9. The following reply was received under date of September 15, 1961:

> We have had a number of inquiries on the letter of General G. G. Meade to General R. E. Lee on the morning of April 9. Unfortunately, we do not have it and have no inkling as to where it may be or whether it exists.
>
> Very sincerely yours, R. N. Williams, 2nd,
> Director.

It appears from this letter that a number of people have tried to track down this illusory note. In the light of the available evidence, it seems doubtful that such a note ever existed. If it ever existed, it does not seem to have been delivered to General Lee.

At the suggestion of Meade, Lee wrote another letter to Grant in the hope that it might reach the Union commander sooner than the one which had been sent through Meade's lines. This letter would be sent through Sheridan's front and was as follows:

> Headquarters, Army of Northern Virginia
> April 9, 1865
>
> Lieut. Gen. U. S. Grant
> Commanding U. S. Armies:
>
> General:
>
> I sent a communication to you to-day from the picket-line, whither I had gone in hopes of meeting you in pursuance of the request contained in my letter of yesterday. Major-General Meade informs me that it would probably expedite matters to send a duplicate through some other part of your lines. I therefore request an interview, at such time and place as you may designate, to discuss the terms of the surrender of this army in accordance with your offer to have such an interview, contained in your letter of yesterday.
>
> Very respectfully, your obedient servant,
> R. E. LEE
> General[130]

This letter went a little further than Lee's earlier letter to Grant. It specified that Lee would be willing to have an interview "at such time and place as you may designate". In his second letter, Lee had offered to meet Grant "between the picket lines of the two armies", which would have been on neutral territory. Now he says, in effect, that he is willing to meet Grant in enemy territory, if necessary, in order to arrange a surrender.

Horace Porter said that Grant received this letter some little time after he received Lee's earlier letter. It was delivered to Grant by Colonel F. C. Newhall, Sheridan's adjutant general, about five or six miles from

Appomattox Court House. According to Porter's account, it was considered merely a duplicate of Lee's earlier letter and did not bring forth any comment from Grant and his party.[131] It is interesting, however, that Grant had already sent word that he was willing to meet Lee at any place where Lee wished to have an interview. On this point, the two commanders were equally courteous.

LEE'S LETTER REQUESTING A SUSPENSION OF HOSTILITIES

Sometime during the morning of April 9, Lee wrote a letter to Grant asking for a suspension of hostilities. It was as follows:

April 9, 1865

Lieut. Gen. U. S. Grant,
Commanding U. S. Armies

General:

I ask a suspension of hostilities pending the adjustment of the terms of surrender of this army, in the interview requested in my former communication to-day.

Very respectfully, your obedient servant,
R. E. LEE
General[132]

Freeman thought that this letter was sent through the Union lines by way of one of the Union couriers who advanced under a flag of truce and asked Lee to withdraw because of an impending attack.[133] In his official report, Meade said: "At the same time (12 M.) I received a letter from General Lee asking for a suspension of hostilities pending negotiations for surrender."[134] Since the letter quoted above seems to be the letter which Meade received at 12 M., it appears that it was probably sent through the lines in some other way than that suggested by Freeman. If it was sent through the lines before Lee left Longstreet's rear, it does not seem reasonable that it would have taken an hour or more to reach Meade, who by this time had moved close to his front.

GRANT'S FOURTH LETTER TO LEE

Shortly before noon on April 9, Lieutenant Charles E. Pease overtook Grant and his party some four miles west of Walker's church. Pease had with him Lee's third letter, the one in which Lee had offered to surrender the Army of Northern Virginia. Sylvanus Cadwallader said that Rawlins first opened and read the note without a word of comment. Then he handed it to Grant, who read it through mechanically and handed it back to Rawlins with the comment: "You had better read it aloud, General." Rawlins drew a long breath and read it in a deep voice. After a period of silence, somebody proposed three cheers, but the cheering was rather feeble and soon changed into tears. They all felt that the war was over. Presently Grant turned to Rawlins and asked: "How will that do, Rawlins?" Rawlins replied: "I think *that* will do." Then Ely S. Parker, the Indian military secretary on Grant's staff, was directed to write the following letter to General Lee:[135]

Headquarters Armies of the U. S.
April 9, 1865

General R. E. Lee
Commanding C. S. Army:

Your note of this date is but of this moment (11:50 A.M.) received. In consequence of my having passed from the Richmond and Lynchburg road to the Farmville and Lynchburg road I am at this writing about four miles west of Walker's church, and will push forward to the front for the purpose of meeting you. Notice sent on this road where you wish the interview to take place will meet me.

Very respectfully, your obedient servant,
U. S. GRANT,
Lieutenant-General[136]

Grant had been suffering from a headache since the night before. Grant said: "When the officer reached me I was still suffering with the sick-headache; but the instant I saw the contents of the note (from Lee) I was cured."[137]

Grant's reply was entrusted to Brevet Brigadier General Orville E. Babcock and his orderly, who were instructed to carry the letter to Lee by the shortest possible route. In Freeman's account, Babcock is called a Lieutenant-Colonel,[138] but his military record shows that he was appointed a Brevet Brigadier General on March 13, 1865.[139] In his *Memoirs,* Grant referred to Babcock as "General Babcock."[140]

Babcock found General Lee seated under the famous apple tree near Appomattox Court House but the time when Lee first arrived at the apple tree seems to be rather uncertain. A discussion of the apple tree and its connection with the surrender is given in a separate section of this study.

Freeman stated that General Lee "remained near the rear of Longstreet's position until after 11 o'clock . . .".[141]

If Lee had stayed in the rear of Longstreet's corps until after 11:00, he would have had very little time at the apple tree. Alexander estimated that Lee sat for "perhaps two hours" under the apple tree.[142] J. W. Hallam said that Lee was "seated for a long time" under the apple tree.[143]

The evidence on this point indicates that Lee must have been at the apple tree at least by 11:00 A.M., as stated in one of the accounts by E. P. Alexander.[144]

Also, there is some evidence that Lee did not go to the apple tree immediately after he returned from Longstreet's rear. Colonel Marshall said that Lee rode "right up in front of Appomattox Court House" in order to stop Fitzhugh Lee's activities and tell him not to fight any more.[145]

Another Confederate, Captain W. N. McDonald, said that Lee also had to make a personal appeal to the men in Harris' Mississippi brigade to get them to cease firing.

> When Harris' Mississippi brigade, of Mahone's division, were informed of the surrender, and ordered to cease firing, most of the officers and men refused to obey, declaring that they would never surrender. Mahone went and expostulated with them, but they would not listen to him. Finally Lee came and made a personal appeal. For some time even his authority was disregarded. Many of the officers and men gathered around him and implored him not to put upon them such disgrace. With tears they begged him to trust himself to their care, swearing that they could and would carry him through safely, and telling him that once in the mountains he could raise another army.[146]

While there may be some doubt about the authenticity of these incidents, such reports do indicate the possibility of at least some activity by Lee on Gordon's front, following his return from Longstreet's rear.

Although no final judgment seems possible, Lee might have written two notes to Grant after he returned to the apple tree, the one requesting a suspension of hostilities and the other being a duplicate of his letter offering to surrender his army.[147]

Colonel T. M. R. Talcott said that Lee talked to him at the apple tree and told him that he considered it his duty to go to see General Grant and to stop further sacrifice of life.[148]

Sheridan sent Brigadier General James W. Forsyth to Meade to ascertain whether a truce between the two armies would be respected. Forsyth saw Lee at the apple tree and asked him for permission to pass through the Confederate lines, which was the shortest route. Lee readily gave his permission and sent Colonel Walter H. Taylor to accompany Forsyth. Taylor said that he went only as far as the Union outposts, while Forsyth entered the Union lines in search of General Meade.[149]

Morris Schaff said that Longstreet wanted some word sent to Humphreys about the truce to keep him from attacking the Confederate rear at New Hope Church, and that it was in accordance with Longstreet's desire that Sheridan sent Forsyth to Meade.[150]

When Forsyth and Taylor returned, Forsyth doubtless had with him a letter from Meade authorizing a truce until 2:00 P.M.

Headquarters Army of the Potomac,
April 9, 1865 - 12 m.

General R. E. Lee:

I have no authority to suspend hostilities unless it is with the distinct understanding that you are prepared to accept the terms indicated in the letter to Lieutenant General Grant sent to you yesterday. I understand General Grant did not accede to your proposition for an interview. Your letter will be at once forwarded to Lieutenant-General Grant and perhaps I may be sooner advised by him if you have had any communications with other parts of our line. I am now advised by General Forsyth that a cessation of hostilities has been agreed upon between your command and General Ord. Under these circumstances, to enable General Forsyth to return and report my action, I agree to a suspension of hostilities till 2 p.m. this day and shall be glad to prolong it on being advised by you that you agree to General Grant's terms.

Respectfully, your obedient servant,
Geo. G. Meade,
Major-General, U. S. Army.[151]

Longstreet said that he talked to Lee under the apple tree and encouraged him to believe that Grant would not impose terms of undue severity.[152]

Freeman thought that Babcock arrived with Grant's letter about 12:15 P.M.,[153] but this seems much too early. Grant did not write his letter until after 11:50 A.M. because Grant said that he received Lee's letter at that time. It probably took fifteen minutes to prepare a reply and start Babcock on his way. E. P. Alexander said that it "was about one o'clock when Babcock came from the enemy's line".[154] 1:00 P.M. seems to be much closer to the time of Babcock's arrival than 12:15 P.M.

Babcock and his orderly were accompanied by a Confederate officer, thought to be Colonel John Fairfax.[155] One report said that Babcock approached the apple tree quite rapidly.

At the first sound of his approach Lee stood erect and awaited his arrival. The officer dismounted at some distance, and, leaving his horse in charge of the aid, advanced toward Lee with head uncovered, and stopping every few paces, bowed repeatedly low to the ground.[156]

While Babcock was undoubtedly courteous, it is not believed that he went to the extreme mentioned by Hallam in showing his respect for General Lee. Colonel W. H. Taylor said that Babcock merely saluted the Confederate commander.[157]

Horace Porter said that Babcock handed Grant's letter to one of Lee's staff officers.[158] Marshall[159] and Taylor[160] stated that Babcock handed the letter to Lee directly. Their version seems to be more acceptable than Porter's. Sylvanus Cadwallader said that Babcock was standing very close to Lee when Lee borrowed a pencil from someone to write on the envelope the time of its receipt. After he had used the pencil, Lee handed it back over his shoulder and Babcock reached for it and carried it away as a souvenir. Later on, Cadwallader succeeded in getting the point of the pencil, about an inch long, as a souvenir for himself.[161] Since Babcock was so close to Lee when he opened Grant's letter, it appears that the letter must have passed directly from Babcock to Lee.

Horace Porter stated that Lee requested Babcock to send a note to Meade asking him to maintain the truce until positive orders could be received from General Grant. He said that Babcock's note was sent through the confederate lines and was carried by a Union officer, accompanied by one of Lee's officers.[162]

Although Porter was mistaken about many things, it appears that his account is substantially correct at this point. Meade stated in his official report that at 2 P.M. he "received the instructions of the lieutenant-general commanding to continue the armistice until further orders."[163] This was probably Babcock's note, which he evidently signed with Grant's name. There does not seem to be any record of the names of the two officers who carried this communication to Meade.

Lee apparently did not read Babcock's note and did not know its content, because he later asked Grant to notify Meade about the surrender in order to prevent the outbreak of renewed hostilities.[164]

FLAGS OF TRUCE

After he had gone to Longstreet's rear in the hope of meeting Grant, General Lee remembered that he had not notified Gordon about the suspension of hostilities and had not authorized Gordon and Longstreet to send out a flag of truce, pending the surrender. He evidently sent a written message to Longstreet by the courier who had brought the report that Fitz Lee was mistaken about a road of escape being open to the army.[165]

Upon receipt of this message, Longstreet sent Captain R. M. Sims forward with a flag of truce, which Sims said was a white crash towel he had purchased in Richmond, for $20 or $40, a few days before the city was evacuated. He rode to Gordon and informed him that a flag of truce had been authorized, whereupon Gordon asked him to carry the flag into the Union lines. Since the Union cavalry was about to envelop the Confederate left, Sims rode in that direction. He soon came in contact with two or three Union officers, who escorted him to Custer, because

Sheridan was not immediately available. Custer told Sims that only an unconditional surrender would be accepted but he did agree to let Sims carry the message back to the Confederate lines, accompanied by two Union officers, Lieutenant-Colonel E. W. Whitaker and Major George G. Briggs.[166]

Sims said that he returned to Gordon with the two Union officers. Gordon asked Sims to carry the flag of truce in another direction, but Sims refused on the ground that he had to return to Longstreet. Sims thought that Gordon then sent a Major Brown to carry the flag.[167]

Gordon gave a somewhat different account. He did not mention Sims at all but said that he sent Colonel Green Peyton with a flag of truce to find Sheridan. Peyton is supposed to have returned with Custer, who demanded an unconditional surrender.[168] In view of the untrustworthiness of Gordon's account of the events at Appomattox, this report cannot be accepted as accurate.

Gordon said that he later sent a "ragged private" along with Vanderbilt Allen, of Sheridan's staff, to stop the firing by some of the men in Gary's Cavalry Brigade.[169] Instead of a ragged private, Colonel W. W. Blackford said that he was the one who was assigned by Gordon to accompany Allen.[170]

Following the presentation of the flag of truce from the Confederate side, Custer rode into the Confederate lines with a flag of truce.[171] He was soon followed by Sheridan, who was accompanied by a body of some thirty or forty horsemen.[172] Sheridan was fired on as he rode into the Confederate lines and had to find shelter in a ravine as he made his way to the Court House.[173]

A flag of truce first came through the Confederate lines on the right of the Union line. The next one evidently came in on Chamberlain's front, which was the infantry fartherest on the right. Chamberlain, as he usually did, gave a very dramatic description of this event:

> Suddenly rose to sight another form, close in our own front, - a soldierly young figure, I see the white flag earnestly borne, and its possible purport sweeps before my inner vision like a wrath of morning mist. He comes steadily on, the mysterious form in gray, my mood so whimsically sensitive that I could even smile at the material of the flag, - wondering where in either army was found a towel, and one so white. But it bore a mighty message, - that simple emblem of homely service, wafted hitherward above the dark and crimsoned streams that never can wash themselves away.
>
> The messenger draws near, dismounts; with graceful salutation of hardly suppressed emotion delivers his message:

"Sir, I am from General Gordon. General Lee desires a cessation of hostilities until he can hear from General Grant as to the proposed surrender."

What word is this! So long so dearly fought for, so feverishly dreamed, but ever snatched away, held hidden and aloof; now smiting the senses with a dizzy flash! "Surrender"? It takes a moment to gather one's speech. "Sir," I answer, "that matter exceeds my authority. I will send to my superior. General Lee is right. He can do no more." All this with a forced calmness, covering a tumult of heart and brain. I bid him wait a while, and the message goes up to my corps commander, General Griffin, leaving me mazed at the boding change.[174]

Chamberlain identified this Confederate officer as "Capt. P. M. Jones, now U. S. District Judge in Alabama."[175] He was mistaken about Jones' initials, which were T. G. instead of P. M.[176]

Jones said that he was not quite 21 years old, was mounted on a good-looking bay horse, and was wearing his best uniform. He rode in on the right of Appomattox Court House and his flag of truce was a white napkin in which some ladies had wrapped a snack for him the day before.[177]

Jones mentioned Sims as the one who carried a flag of truce from Longstreet to Gordon to Custer. He also named a Captain or Major Arnold, who was serving under C. A. Evans, and Major Hunter, of Gordon's staff,[178] as others who carried flags of truce.

Chamberlain said there was so much confusion about the various flags of truce that sometimes he had to go back and read the official records to make himself believe that he was present at Appomattox at all. He thought that at least ten flags were sent out by Longstreet and Gordon.

The flag that came to me I sent along the line to the left to Sheridan and Ord. Of course, it passed many commands and commanders, and so all these stories of receiving this "flag of truce" may well be true. The flag came to me first. There is no doubt about that, and I sent it along. It was from Longstreet and Gordon. It was the identical flag that went to Sheridan. If there were other flags, I do not know who sent them. Grant was not on the field then.[179]

After Jones had left, Chamberlain saw two others ride up with flags of truce. One was E. W. Whitaker of Custer's staff and the other was a Captain Brown of Georgia.[180] The latter was evidently the Major Brown to whom Sims referred. Chamberlain said:

Without dismounting, without salutation, the cavalryman

(Whitaker) shouts: "This is unconditional surrender: This is the end!" Then he hastily introduces his companion, and adds: "I am just from Gordon and Longstreet. Gordon says 'For God's sake, stop this infantry, or hell will be to pay!' I'll go to Sheridan," he adds, and dashes away with the white flag, leaving Longstreet's aide with me.

I was doubtful of my duty. The flag of truce was in, but I had no right to act upon it without orders. There was still some firing from various quarters, lulling a little where the white flag passed near. But I did not press things quite so hard.[181]

In regard to the claim that the last man killed was in the Army of the James, Chamberlain said that it might "possibly be so, as the reception of flags began on our right, and probably did not reach the extreme left where the Army of the James was until some time after. So there may have been some firing and casualties after the truce had been received on our right. The honor of this last death is not a proper subject of quarrel."[182]

Chamberlain believed that it was about ten o'clock on the morning of April 9 when the flags of truce appeared and firing died down on his front.[183] This time appears to be approximately correct.[184]

The evidence indicates that a number of Confederates raised flags of truce on their own initiative at various points along the line. Brevet Colonel J. B. Pattee said that as his men were entering the village of Appomattox Court House a flag of truce came through his lines. Despite the flag of truce, he claimed that some Confederates continued to fire from the cover of the houses, killing a cavalryman, and that his men swept on through the village.[185]

Perhaps the last flag of truce on the morning of April 9 was sent out under Union auspices. Munford's cavalry had swung around the Union left and struck the Lynchburg road some little distance west of the Court House. This caused a body of Union cavalry to be between them and the Court House. The news that hostilities had been suspended came through the Union lines and was relayed to Munford under a Union flag of truce. As reported by Colonel S. B. M. Young, "General Davies sent flag of truce and a cessation of hostilities was agreed upon."[186]

Captain M. J. Billmyer, of the First Virginia Cavalry, said that this flag of truce came into the Confederate lines between 11 and 12 o'clock.[187]

CUSTER'S DEMAND FOR UNCONDITIONAL SURRENDER

When Captain R. M. Sims, carrying a white towel as a Confederate flag of truce, rode into the Union lines on the morning of April 9, he first asked for Major General P. H. Sheridan, but since Sheridan was not close by, he was referred to Bvt. Major General G. A. Custer.

Sims wrote the following account of his conversation with Custer:

> He (Custer) asked: "Who are you, and what do you wish?" I replied: "I am of General Longstreet's staff, but am the bearer of a message from General Gordon to General Sheridan, asking for a suspension of hostilities until General Lee can be heard from, who has gone down the road to meet General Grant to have a conference." General Custer replied: "We will listen to no terms but that of unconditional surrender. We are behind your army now and it is at our mercy." I replied: "You will allow me to carry this message back?" He said: "Yes." "Do you wish to send an officer with me?" Hesitating a little, he said: "Yes," and directed the two officers who came with me, Lieutenant-Colonel Whitaker, and the major, whose name I don't know, to go with me. We rode back to Gordon in almost a straight line.[188]

Soon after Sims left the Union lines on his way back to Gordon, he said that Custer and an orderly rode into the Confederate lines. Custer borrowed a handkerchief from his orderly and tied it to his saber as a flag of truce. When Custer reached the Confederate lines, some of the Confederates gave the orderly some rough treatment and were about to treat Custer the same way, but he was rescued by an old West Point friend, W. H. Gibbes.[189]

There can be no doubt that Custer did ride into the Confederate lines soon after the flag of truce was first presented by the Confederates. Contemporary newspaper reports and other sources all testify to his presence inside the Confederate lines.[190]

Even Custer's defenders admit that he made a dash into the Confederate lines. In *The Custer Story,* Marguerite Merington did not deny that Custer made this venture but she qualified her statement by saying that he "returned almost immediately."[191]

The controversial point is the conversation which took place between Custer and Longstreet. The wife of Custer became very much annoyed by the story that her husband asked Longstreet for the Army of Northern Virgina to be surrendered unconditionally. She wrote to Captain Michael V. Sheridan, the brother of P. H. Sheridan, and asked him to state the precise facts about this incident. Captain Sheridan obligingly wrote to Mrs. Custer and denied that Custer ever demanded the surrender of the Army of Northern Virginia.[192]

Although he did not deny that Custer demanded of Longstreet the surrender of the Army of Northern Virginia, Jay Monaghan objected to several versions of this incident, especially the report that Longstreet tried to bluff Custer by threatening to have Pickett deploy his division and wipe out Custer's division. He also questioned Gordon's statement that Custer asked Gordon for the immediate and unconditional surrender of all the troops under his command.[193]

It seems that Monaghan's objections have considerable weight. As he points out, Custer probably knew what had happened to Pickett's troops at Five Forks and would not have been scared by a threat from Longstreet to throw them into action.

In the light of the account by Captain R. M. Sims, the statement of Gordon about his conversation with Custer seems very doubtful. Sims said that he rode directly from Custer to Gordon. When he left Gordon and went to Longstreet, he found Custer talking with Longstreet. This account does not indicate that there was any time when Custer might have talked to Gordon.[194]

Further doubt is cast on Gordon's story by his own earlier account of the events at Appomattox. In that account he said that "some one representing General Sheridan" approached him with a demand for surrender. He did not mention the Union officer's name but referred to him as a "Major", which was not in keeping with Custer's rank.[195]

This unidentified Union major, mentioned by Gordon, was apparently the major who accompanied Sims on his ride back from Custer.[196] Sims said that he did not remember his name but he has been identified as Major George G. Briggs of the 7th Michigan Cavalry.[197]

Freeman accepted Gordon's later version of this affair. He did not comment on the difference between Gordon's two accounts and might not have noticed the variation.[198]

F. M. Colston said that he saw Custer approach Longstreet and have a conversation with him. He stated that bystanders were waved aside and that all he knew about the incident was what he was told immediately afterwards. Custer was reported to have demanded the surrender of the army, and when Longstreet refused he said that Longstreet would be responsible for the bloodshed to follow. Longstreet replied that he could "go ahead and have all the bloodshed he wanted." Custer then learned that General Lee had gone to see General Grant, and mounted his horse and rode off.[199]

Captain R. M. Sims said that Custer and Longstreet were already talking by the time he reached them, and he evidently did not hear very much of their conversation. He said that he heard Custer say that he would proceed to attack at once and that Longstreet replied: "As soon as you please."[200]

Freeman referred to four accounts of this incident, written by Longstreet, Alexander, J. C. Haskell, and W. M. Owen, and said that he preferred the narratives of Alexander and Haskell, "both of whom were young men, apt to remember the details of so sensational an affair."[201] Judging by his summary, Freeman believed that Custer did demand an unconditional surrender from Longstreet and that Longstreet roughly ordered Custer to return to his own lines. Longstreet's exact language may be doubtful but it seems reasonable to believe that Custer did demand an unconditional surrender and that his demand met with a firm refusal from Longstreet.

CONFERENCE OF CAVALRY OFFICERS ALONG STAGE ROAD

Munford's Cavalry was on the right of the Confederate line on the morning of April 9. When the attack began, Munford's men made a detour around the Union left, skirmishing along the way. After going perhaps a mile, they began to bear to their own left and struck the Richmond-Lynchburg Stage Road at the top of a considerable hill some distance west of the Court House.[202]

The Confederate cavalry was charged by the Union troopers, and there was considerable skirmishing, with some casualties being inflicted. S. B. M. Young, a Union colonel of the 4th Pennsylvania Cavalry, said he then heard that there had been a suspension of hostilities and sent a courier along the road, with a white handkerchief tied to a saber, to inform Munford that negotiations were going on for a surrender and that the Federal officers wished to have a conference with him. Munford is said to have raised his hand and exclaimed, "my God, is that so?"[203]

On the previous evening, one of Munford's subordinates had stopped at his home in the vicinity and had obtained two flasks of fine old peach brandy. He had presented one flask to Munford, and Munford had taken a generous swallow. The odor was on his breath when he came together with Davies, Crook, MacKenzie, and Young for a conference. Munford stated that he could not "speak with authority" about surrendering unless he was allowed to communicate with Confederate headquarters.

In the meantime, one of the officers in the circle remarked with a smile that he noticed "the proximity of a damned good Spring". Munford's flask was then passed around and was finally returned to him empty of its contents.

Munford stated that he did not think he should surrender his command and said that it was his intention to leave along the Lynchburg road as best he could.

The brandy had probably added something to the congeniality of the group, because the Union officers agreed that the Confederates would be allowed to ride away unmolested. S. B. M. Young wrote:

> The general impression among our officers that morning of April 9th '65 was that you had made a good fight and were entitled to the credit of carrying your Cavalry Division out of the chaos.[204]

Young said that Davies was the senior Union officer present at this conference and that Munford talked with Davies in the presence of the other officers. This evidently means that Davies was chiefly responsible for the decision to allow Munford and his men to ride away unmolested. In his official report, Young said that Davies "sent flag of truce and a cessation of hostilities was agreed upon."[205]

Munford wrote to MacKenzie on April 17 saying that he had tried to communicate with General R. E. Lee on April 9 but that Devin would not allow him to do so. "I shall follow our old flag and defend it until we are free," was his defiant statement.[206] However, Brevet Brigadier General J. I. Gregg reported that Munford was paroled at Lynchburg on April 20.[207] Gibbon informed Munford on April 21 that the question of the actual escape of his command would be left to Munford's decision.[208]

Captain M. J. Billmyer, of the First Virginia Cavalry, said that the Union pickets had been instructed not to shoot at anyone on the night of April 9 and that he, Colonels Woolridge and Morgan, Lieutenant W. N. Lemen, and many others slipped away that night. He said that these men had formed Munford's rearguard and did not leave with the majority of Munford's troopers.[209]

It should be noted here that there is a difference of opinion about whether or not Munford was ever a general in the Confederate Army, since he was not actually appointed a general by President Jefferson Davis.

Freeman defended Munford's right to be called a general and listed him as Brigadier General Thomas T. Munford, C. S. A.[210] In doing this, Freeman lined up against the partisans of Major General T. L. Rosser, who asserted that Munford had no right to the title of general.

Ezra J. Warner, one of the most recent writers on this subject, took the position that Munford was never a general and that his name should not be included among the individuals who received appointment by President Davis to one of the four grades of general. Warner said: "In their (D. B. Harris, T. T. Munford, H. K. Douglas) cases it was the obvious wish of their superior officers that they receive promotion to brigadier - but apparently *not* the intention of President Davis."[211]

THE CONFERENCE AT THE COURT HOUSE

Soon after the suspension of hostilities on the morning of April 9, a group of Union and Confederate officers came together for a conference in front of the old Court House building. Because of the more significant conference which was held later in the day at the McLean House, this earlier conference has been largely overlooked and is seldom mentioned in Civil War histories.

References to this conference are found in the writings of several of those who were present. John Gibbon said:

> I dismounted, and, with many other officers, loitered about the square, anxiously waiting to hear the result of the negotiations. All war-like sounds had ceased, but both parties had picket lines out in front. The town was between the two, and prominent officers on both sides, who had not met, except in battle, for four years, mingled together and chatted about the coming event. All wore an air of anxiety, but all seemed hopeful that there would be no further necessity for bloodshed.
>
> Here I again met Longstreet, last seen between the picket-lines in front of Richmond, and General Henry Heth, an old friend and classmate with whom I had last shaken hands nearly five years before at Camp Floyd in far-distant Utah. . . .
>
> While we were thus waiting, some one said, "There is Cadmus." Looking up, I saw General Wilcox, another classmate, riding into the square on a sorry-looking gray horse whose thin ribs bespoke the scant forage on which he had been subsisting. The rider was dressed in a long, thick overcoat, and after he had dismounted and saluted the group of officers, I asked him if he was cold, that he wore an overcoat. He grimly replied, "It's all I have"; and opening the coat, he showed us that a shirt was the only garment underneath. Pointing to a pair of bags on his saddle, he said, "That's all the baggage I have left," and turning to General Sheridan, he remarked: "You have captured all the rest, and you can't have *that* till you capture me." Heth was dressed in a new suit of Confederate gray, and accounted for the fact by saying that, when he found we were capturing all their baggage, he concluded to put on all his good clothes, and save them till the end in preference to the old ones.[212]

Cadmus Wilcox said that he talked with Sheridan about the existence of a flag of truce and that both commanders agreed to withdraw their troops from their advanced positions.

> I rode back at once to the Court House, to send orders to my brigades to withdraw back to the road. Soon a number of Federal officers joined us, among them many that I knew; Gen. Gibbon, Gen. Griffin, Gen. Merritt, Gen. Ayres and others; one

of the Generals, Gibbon, proposed that in the event Gens. Lee and Grant did not come to terms and stop it, that we should in future require our men to load with blank cartridges, and so that no more of them might be killed.[213]

This statement by Wilcox agrees with the one already quoted from Gibbon, in which Gibbon said that "all seemed hopeful that there would be no further necessity for bloodshed."

Major General E. O. C. Ord hardly mentioned the conference at the Court House. He merely referred to the fact that he talked to Gordon after the surrender and that Gordon told him that General Lee would not believe him when he said that Ord's army was in his front.[214]

Major General Wesley Merritt also gave a very brief description of the conference at the Court House.

Then came the truce, and it was agreed that there should be no more fighting until, I think, two o'clock. The officers met and talked over old times. I saw many Confederates whom I had known at West Point. When we parted, about two o'clock, they all expressed regret that the "incident could not be closed at once," and were sad, they said, that fighting must continue. We knew that they had no chance, and thought that they knew it too.[215]

J. L. Chamberlain wrote about the Court House conference:

A truce is agreed upon until one o'clock, - it is now ten. A conference is to be held, - or rather colloquy, for no one here is authorized to say anything about the terms of surrender. Six or eight officers from each side meet between the lines, near the courthouse, waiting Lee's answer to Grant's summons to surrender. There is lively chat here on this unaccustomed opportunity for exchange of notes and queries.

The first greetings are not all so dramatic as might be thought, for so grave an occasion, "Well, Billy, old boy, how goes it?" asks one loyal West Pointer of a classmate he had been fighting for four years. "Bad, bad, Charlie, bad I tell you; but have you got any whisky?" was the response - not poetic - not idealistic, but historic; founded on fact as to the strength of the demand, but without evidence of the questionable maxim that the demand creates the supply. More of the economic truth was manifest that scarcity enhances value.

Everybody seems acquiescent, and for the moment cheerful, - except Sheridan. He does not like the cessation of hostilities, and does not conceal his opinion. His natural disposition was not sweetened by the circumstances that he

> was fired on by some of the Confederates as he was coming up to the meeting under the truce. He is for unconditional surrender and thinks we should have banged right on and settled all questions without asking them. He strongly intimates that some of the free-thinking rebel cavalry might take advantage of the truce to get away from us. But the Confederate officers, one and all, Gordon, Wilcox, Heth, "Rooney" Lee, and all the rest assure him of their good faith, and that the game is up for them.[216]

Morris Schaff said:

> I will not cumber the narrative with all that happened in the next hour and a half at the Court-House; let it suffice that Longstreet, Wilcox, Heth and other West Pointers from the South, joined Ord, Sheridan, Griffin, Custer and Pennington from the North, in the friendliest spirit, and agreed to wait till Grant and Lee had met.[217]

Since other reports do not mention that Custer and Pennington were at the Court House conference, Schaff's statement cannot be accepted without verification from other sources.

There is one other report that mentions Custer at the Court House. This is in Augustus Buell's *The Cannoneer,* a book which is fraudulent in many respects and is completely untrustworthy.[218] Along with Custer, Buell included Grant, Meade, Humphreys, Wright, and thirty or forty others.[219]

Adam Badeau was not among those present at the Court House conferences but he did write a brief description of it.

> Sheridan rode over to Appomattox court-house, and there met Generals Gordon and Wilcox of the rebel army, who informed him that negotiations for a surrender were pending between Grant and Lee. Sheridan, however, declared that, if this were so, the attack upon his lines with a view to escape should not have been made, and he must have some assurance that a surrender was intended. This Gordon personally gave, and an agreement was made to meet again in half an hour. At the specified time a second interview was had, Ord and Longstreet now accompanying Sheridan and Gordon; and Longstreet repeated the assurance that Lee intended to surrender, and was only awaiting the arrival of Grant. Hostilities then ceased until the general-in-chief rode up.[220]

The most complete descriptions of the conference at the Court House are found in some contemporary newspaper dispatches. The following is from the New York *Freeman's Journal and Catholic Register* of April 22, 1865:

CONFERENCE BETWEEN ORD AND LONGSTREET

In the meantime General Ord, accompanied by his staff and bodyguard, had ridden down to the outskirts of the Appomattox, where he left his party, and attended by only a few, advanced towards the Court House and met General Longstreet and several other Confederate officers.

THE PARTIES PRESENT

The parties present at this historical conference were, on the Union side, Generals Ord, Sheridan, Gibbon, Merritt, Ayres, Griffin, Bartlett, and Crook; Colonel Small, Chief Commissary, and Surgeon Mott, Medical Inspector of the Army of the James. On the rebel side were Generals Longstreet, Gordon, Heth, Wilcox, Fairfax and Surgeon Cullan.

THE MEETING

General Ord, as soon as Longstreet approached, advanced, and was introduced to him by General Sheridan. They immediately retired together, and had a long and apparently very interesting conversation, while the other members of the party on both sides fraternized in small throngs, and discussed the affairs of the Conference and the contents of the various flasks that had been brought out especially for the occasion. The two principal generals, I have since discovered, were unable to make any terms, as the whole power of settling the matter rested with Grant and Lee. Longstreet informed General Ord that Lee was already communicating with Grant, and that undoubtedly something would come of it. It was arranged that hostilities should not be resumed, and no troops should be moved from their positions on either side until due and timely notice should be given General Ord by General Longstreet.

THE OUTSIDE CONVERSATION

During all this time General Gordon, of Longstreet's command, was giving many interesting particulars to the party accompanying General Ord. He stated that the Confederacy was about played out. He said that the only hope Lee had was to break through our lines and take the Lynchburg Road. At a council of war held in the rebel lines yesterday, General Lee had stated that he did not believe anything was between him and the road but Sheridan's cavalry. He said that he did not believe infantry could have made that heavy march of forty miles from Farmville in little over twenty-four hours, and furthermore he added that he had intercepted a dispatch to move on Appomattox Court House, and he felt confident that as the latter had not received the order he had not moved. Unfortunately General Lee had not calculated on Ord moving the moment he heard that Sheridan had struck the enemy, with or without orders, neither had he properly estimated the character of these iron men, who, under Gibbon and Griffin, had pressed forward with an endurance and rapidity hardly surpassed by the cavalry itself. General Gordon informed our officers that he had not agreed with Lee in his opinion, and that from the first he was satisfied that Ord was in their front. His view, however, was overruled, and Lee made his attack this morning on the cavalry only to find behind their retreating ranks a line of bristling bayonets impossible to break. When this admission of the rebel general spread through our lines, the officers and men for the first time properly appreciated the great importance of our late extraordinary forced marches. If the column of infantry had arrived an hour later Lee would have broken through Sheridan and formed a line across the Lynchburg road, where a severe battle position on the side of the enemy, who could have moved their trains along their rear and then followed them.

GENERAL ORD RETURNS

After a lengthly conversation with Longstreet, General Ord parted from him, and accompanied by his party, returned to our lines; General Longstreet, on his part, riding back to his men. During the whole conference innumerable field glasses had been levelled at the party from both armies.

The same New York newspaper contained another description of the conference at the Court House written by L. A. Hendrick.

CONFERENCES OF COMMANDING OFFICERS

A conference of commanding officers of both sides was soon held, the place of preliminary conference was on the steps of the court house. On our side were Generals Ord, Sheridan, Crook, Gibbon, Griffin, Merritt, Ayres, Bartlett, Chamberlain, Forsyth and Michie. On the enemy's side were Generals Longstreet, Gordon, Heth, Wilcox, Colonel Fairfax and other officers. The conference lasted some hour and a half. It was a singular spectacle. I stood on our skirmish line, none but general officers being allowed to pass through the line, and had a full view of the group. There were mutual introductions and shaking of hands, and soon was passed about some whiskey (General Ayres furnished the whiskey and he alleges that it was a first class article) and mutual healths were drank and altogether it was a strange grouping. The rebel officers were all elegantly dressed in full uniform. Gradually the area of the conference widened. From the steps the conferring party got into the street, and before it closed some were seated on the steps, and others, for lack of more comfortable accommodations, chatted cosily, seated on a contiguous fence. As stated above, the former interview was only preliminary. This time of remaining together was spent waiting the arrival of Lieutenant-General Grant and an interview between the latter and General Lee. Lieutenant-General Grant was miles away, and the conference ended as between the parties named.

From these various accounts of the conference at the Court House, it appears that the Union and Confederate officers manifested a very friendly spirit toward one another; they all hoped that there would be no more bloodshed; Longstreet and Ord agreed that all hostilities would be suspended and that there would be no troop movements during the armistice.

This conference on the Court House steps, along the fence, and in the yard was apparently the only significant event connected with the surrender which took place in close proximity to the old Court House building.

An account published in 1866 said:

> While negotiations were being conducted by the two Commanders-in-Chief, the General officers of either army were mingling socially together in the street of Appomattox C. H. and drinking mutual healths. Gens. Ord, Sheridan, Gibbon, Michie and others of the Federals, Gens. Longstreet, Heath (sic), Gordon and others, of the Confederates.[221]

The conference at the Court House broke up before Grant arrived, and there is no evidence that the officers of the two armies were fraternizing while the surrender conference was underway.

THE SURRENDER CONFERENCE

Lee asked both Colonels Charles Marshall and Walter H. Taylor to accompany him to the surrender conference with Grant. Taylor excused himself, however, on the ground that he had already ridden through the lines on two occasions that morning. He admitted that his excuse was rather lame.

> I shrank from this interview, and while I could not then,

> and cannot now, justify my conduct, I availed myself of the excuse of having taken the two rides through the extent of our lines and to those of the enemy, already mentioned, and did not accompany my chief in this trying ordeal.[222]

General Lee had been dressed in a new uniform, with a beautiful sash and sword, ever since 1 A.M. on the morning of April 9. Pendleton described his appearance at the time:

> To my surprise he was dressed in his neatest style, new uniform, snowy linen, etc. On my expressing astonishment at this, considering the hour and circumstances, and asking what it meant, he said, "I have probably to be General Grant's prisoner, and thought I must make my best appearance."[223]

Colonel Charles Marshall thought that he should try to improve his bedraggled appearance before setting out for the conference with Grant. He said that he borrowed a dress sword, a pair of gauntlets, and a clean shirt collar from his friend, Colonel Henry Young.[224] Lee and Marshall both presented a very fine appearance, and their handsome dress later elicited many favorable comments from those who described the surrender conference at the McLean House.

Lee rode to the McLean House, from the vicinity of the apple tree, in company with Colonel Charles Marshall, Sergeant G. W. Tucker, Brevet Brigadier General O. E. Babcock, and Babcock's orderly.[225]

A. C. M. Pennington, a Union cavalry officer, said that he saw Lee and his companions ride across the bridge spanning the Northern Branch of the Appomattox River.[226] Pennington not only saw Lee but Lee spied Pennington, Custer, and a colonel of a North Carolina regiment having a conversation about one hundred and fifty yards downstream.

> General Lee spied us and sent Babcock over to say that he did not wish any communication between the officers or men of the two armies until after he had seen General Grant. We separated at once, having agreed to reconvene as soon as General Lee was out of sight. As soon as they turned a corner of the road, we reassembled and were still chatting when General Lee returned. He had seen Grant.[227]

Colonel Charles Marshall did not mention this incident in his account of the ride to the McLean House. General Lee probably sent Babcock to request Pennington and his companions to break up their conversation while Marshall rode into the village to secure a place for the surrender conference, which would have made it not come under Marshall's observation.

This indicates that Lee dispatched Marshall to find a suitable place for the surrender conference soon after they crossed the bridge. Marshall declared that he was sent forward when they "struck up the hill towards Appomattox Court House."[228]

Freeman conjectured that Babcock and Lee did not talk to each other while they were waiting on Marshall to send word that he found a place for the surrender conference.[229] Since Lee must have spoken to Babcock when he dispatched him to break up Pennington's conversation, and probably discussed his reasons for doing so, it does not seem that Freeman's conjecture is justified.

Marshall was accompanied on his ride into the village by his orderly, Sergeant Tucker. The first white civilian they saw in the village was Major Wilmer McLean, who had moved from the first battle field of Manassas to Appomattox Court House in order to find a place of refuge from armed conflict. Marshall wrote:

> I rode up to him and said, "Can you show me a house where General Lee and General Grant can meet together?" He took me into a house that was all dilapidated and that had no furniture in it. I told him it wouldn't do. Then he said, "Maybe my house will do!" He lived in a very comfortable house, and I told him I thought that would suit. I had taken the orderly along with me, and I sent him back to bring General Lee and Babcock, who were coming on behind. I went into the house and sat down, and after a while General Lee and Babcock came in. Colonel Babcock told his orderly that he was to meet General Grant, who was coming on the road, and turn him in when he came along. So General Lee, Babcock and myself sat down in McLean's parlour and talked in the most friendly and affable way.[230]

Since Babcock never left any written description of his experiences at Appomattox,[231] the account by Marshall is considered the most trustworthy description of this phase of the surrender proceedings.

There are other references which contain different details. General Cullum's *Biographical Register of the Officers and Graduates of the United States Military Academy* gives Babcock the credit for selecting "the place of Meeting of the contending Generals".[232] This statement was repeated in Babcock's obituary notice contained in the *1884 Annual Reunion of the Association of Graduates, West Pont, New York.*[233] These statements may be safely disregarded.

Horace Porter gave General Lee the credit for selecting the place of meeting and said nothing about Marshall's being sent forward for this purpose.[234] This, too, may be safely disregarded.

Marshall entered the left front room or parlour of the McLean House and sat down to wait for the arrival of Lee and Babcock, who soon followed. Marshall estimated that they had to wait for about half an hour on Grant and that during that time they "talked in the most friendly and affable way."[235] For some unknown reason, Freeman decided to disregard Marshall's statement at this point and said: "Half an hour passed, perhaps the longest half hour in Lee's whole life. If there was any conversation, it was in snatches and was slow, labored, and vague." He documented this statement by saying that "Babcock never wrote of Appomattox."[236] The evidence indicates that Babcock was very affable by nature, and there seems to be no reason to believe that Lee found it unusually difficult to carry on a conversation with him. Morris Schaff said: "For a youth with a gentler face or with more of the natural bloom of charity and good-will in it, or with less reprehensive blue eyes, could not have been found in the army."[237]

The Confederate and Union orderlies had been left outside the McLean House. Babcock instructed his orderly to direct Grant to the House whenever he arrived for the surrender conference.[238]

About 1:30 P.M., or perhaps a little later, Grant and his party arrived in the little village of Appomattox Court House. As already noted, Alexander said that Babcock arrived at the apple tree about 1:00 P.M. Marshall stated that he, Babcock, and Lee waited about half an hour for Grant after they arrived at the McLean House. This would make the time between 1:30 and 2:00 in the afternoon.

Grant had followed the Walker's Church, or Prince Edward Court House Road, until he struck the LeGrand road. This he took to the left, went across Plain Run, and entered the Richmond-Lynchburg Stage Road a little to the west of the McLean House.[239]

At the edge of the village, Grant met Sheridan and Ord, who were dismounted and waiting for Grant to appear. Sheridan said that Grant spoke to him first, saying simply, "How are you, Sheridan?" Sheridan assured him that he was "first-rate". Grant then asked: "Is General Lee up there?" Sheridan said: "There is his army down in that valley, and he himself is over in that house (designating McLean's house) waiting to surrender to you." Grant, addressing Ord and Sheridan, said: "Come let us go over." Sheridan and Ord mounted their horses and joined the rest of the cavalcade for the short ride to the McLean House.[240]

There are a number of accounts of what happened when Grant arrived at the McLean House. Marshall, the only Confederate officer in addition to Lee who was present, wrote a detailed account of what took place at the surrender conference. There are, in addition, accounts by Grant, Sheridan, Porter, Parker, Badeau, Sharpe, Merritt, Gibbon, Chamberlain, Cadwallader, G. A. Forsyth, and perhaps others.

The account by Horace Porter is widely quoted and has been accepted by many Civil War historians as a trustworthy account. A discussion of Porter's narrative is included in a separate section of this study. There it is said that Porter's account has so many questionable details that it should be used with extreme caution. Several of the other writers, including Badeau and Forsyth, apparently relied heavily on Porter.

Using the principle that the accounts of the chief participants are generally the most reliable, the narratives of Marshall and Grant are given a higher rating in this study than the accounts by Porter and others. Since it is virtually impossible to note all the differences in the various accounts of the surrender conference, only the ones considered the most important are mentioned here.

Horace Porter said that Babcock saw Grant approaching and opened the door of the room on the left to welcome him to the conference.[241] Although this was not mentioned by Grant and Marshall, it seems likely that Babcock would have performed this act of courtesy.

Porter indicated that Grant first went into the room alone,[242] and this was accepted by Freeman.[243]

Grant said:

> When I went into the house I found General Lee. We greeted each other, and after shaking hands took our seats. I had my staff with me, a good portion of whom were in the room during the whole of the interview.[244]

Marshall likewise stated that Grant had "with him General Sheridan, General Ord, Colonel Badeau, General Porter, Colonel Parker, and quite a number of other officers whose names I do not recall."[245]

Sheridan said: "When I entered McLean's house General Lee was standing, as was also his military secretary, Colonel Marshall, his only staff-officer present."[246]

This is regarded as sufficient evidence that Grant either did not enter the surrender room alone, or was followed almost immediately by his officers. Porter said that Lee did not remember Grant,[247] and this was repeated by Freeman.[248]

Both Grant[249] and Marshall[250] said that Lee did remember Grant. This was accepted by Morris Schaff in *The Sunset of the Confederacy.*[251]

It is presumed that Lee recognized Grant from his association with him in the old army, during their service in Mexico.

Porter said that the Union officers entered the room after Grant sent Babcock to invite them to come in.[252] This was repeated by Freeman.[253]

Sheridan's version of this point is regarded as more correct. He said that the officers entered the room along with Grant, and were introduced to Lee; then some withdrew, and entered again when Grant sent Babcock to invite them to come in.[254]

Grant mentioned that he had a conversation with Lee about their days in the old army.[255] He said that their conversation was so very pleasant that Lee finally had to suggest that they get around to the business of the surrender.[256]

Freeman believed that the Union officers "remained silent in the background" until Grant introduced them to Lee while the surrender letters were being copied.[257]

A contrary opinion was expressed by Colonel Charles Marshall. Colonel Marshall said that "some other Federal officers took part in the conversation" prior to the discussion of the surrender terms and the writing of the surrender letters.[258] While this does not seem to be mentioned elsewhere, it does not appear unlikely that some of Grant's staff did join in the early conversation.

Grant might have needed some assistance from his officers in carrying on his conversation with Lee. He later admitted that he was "sad and depressed" during his interview with Lee and that he "felt like anything rather than rejoicing" on that occasion.[259]

Marshall also seems to be the sole authority for the statement that Lee inquired for General Lawrence Williams in order that he might thank him for sending word about the safety of Custis Lee.[260]

Marshall said Lee brought up the subject of the surrender by saying: "General, I have come to meet you in accordance with my letter to you this morning, to treat about the surrender of my army, and I think the best way would be for you to put your terms in writing." Grant answered, "Yes, I believe it will."[261]

In Grant's account, it is said that when Lee brought up the subject of the surrender, Grant assured him that he merely meant that Lee's army should lay down their arms, not to take them up again during the continuance of the war unless duly and properly exchanged. Lee replied that he had so understood Grant's letter. Grant said that the conversation drifted away from the surrender until Lee suggested that the terms be put in writing.[262]

Although given in slightly different forms, it does not seem that there is any serious disagreement in most of the various accounts on the point that Lee brought up the matter of the surrender and readily agreed to the terms offered by Grant.

There is a Southern account of the conversation between Grant and Lee which is entirely different. According to this version, General Lee opened his conversation with Grant by saying, "General, I deem it due to proper candor and frankness to say at the very beginning of this interview that I am not willing even to discuss any terms of surrender inconsistent with the honor of my army, which I am determined to maintain until the last." General Grant replied: "I have no idea of proposing dishonorable terms, general, but I would be glad if you would state what you consider honorable terms." General Lee then briefly stated the terms upon which he would be willing to surrender. Grant expressed himself as being satisfied whem them, and Lee requested that he would formally reduce the propositions to writing. It was claimed that this was "the substance, and for the most part the exact language, of General Lee's own account of the surrender."[263]

Since this book was not published until after the death of General Lee, he did not have an opportunity to deny the truth of this story. It is not considered worthy of serious consideration. Grant said in his telegram to Stanton at 4:30 P.M. on April 9: "General Lee surrendered the army of Northern Virginia this afternoon on terms proposed by myself."[264] There is really no evidence to disprove this statement.

Freeman said that when Grant started to write out the terms of surrender that he "lit his pipe, puffed furiously".[265] This was a curious error. E. S. Parker, Grant's military secretary, said: "During the entire proceedings Grant had smoked a cigar which he half chewed." Parker said that he had seen Grant on other occasions "smoking very hard, at times completely enveloping his face in the smoke. . . . He smoked in the same manner when, near Appomattox, he received General Lee's last note asking for a meeting with a view to surrender; and again when sitting with Lee in McLean's parlor arranging the terms of surrender."[266]

Most of those who wrote about the surrender conference did not mention Grant's cigar, and the artists who painted it did not include it in their pictures. Perhaps they thought that it would make Grant appear too undignified if he were described or portrayed with a cigar in his mouth.

Another thing about Grant which is seldom mentioned is his field glasses. Thomas Nast of Morristown, New Jersey, completed a picture of the surrender room on April 9, 1895, exactly thirty years after the day of the surrender. While Nast was working on his picture, it is said that he had the advice of Horace Porter and Charles Marshall, and that Marshall was especially helpful in making many suggestions. Cyril Nast, the son of Thomas Nast, modeled for Grant and wore the jacket, boots, and field glasses which Grant wore at the surrender conference.[267] Neither Porter nor Marshall mentioned Grant's field glasses in writing about the surrender, and yet both of them must have told Nast that Grant had his field glasses with him.

When Grant called for his manifold order-book, it was supplied by E.

S. Parker, who said that the book was prepared for three copies.[268]

Grant described the way he wrote down the surrender terms as follows:

> When I put my pen to the paper I did not know the first word that I should make use of in writing the terms. I only knew what was in my mind, and I wished to express it clearly, so that there could be no mistaking it. As I wrote on, the thought occurred to me that the officers had their own private horses and effects, which were important to them, but of no value to us; also that it would be an unnecessary humiliation to call upon them to deliver their side-arms.
>
> No conversation - not one word - passed between General Lee and myself, either about private property, side-arms, or kindred subjects. He appeared to have no objections to the terms first proposed; or, if he had a point to make against them, he wished to wait until they were in writing to make it.[269]

Horace Porter said that Grant paused during his writing and caught sight of Lee's sword, which gave him the idea that it would be an unnecessary humiliation to ask the Confederate officers to surrender their swords, personal baggage, and horses.[270] Adam Badeau claimed that Grant himself confirmed that this was true to the facts.[271] Grant said that the idea of exempting the belongings of officers "did not occur to me until the moment I wrote it down."[272]

After he had finished writing the surrender terms, Grant went over his letter with his military secretary, Ely S. Parker, and together they made a few corrections. Parker perhaps did not remember this phase of the proceedings very well because his biographer quoted Porter's account in regard to this point.[273]

When Grant handed the order-book to Lee, it is said that Lee busied himself with various little acts, such as placing the book on the table near him, taking out his spectacles, wiping them off with his handkerchief, and crossing his legs. Freeman thought that he did these things "as though to master his nerves."[274]

Grant did not think that Lee revealed his feelings to any extent during the surrender conference. Grant said: "What General Lee's feelings were I do not know. . . . Whatever his feelings, they were entirely concealed from my observation".[275]

The letter which Grant handed to Lee was as follows:

> Headquarters, Armies of the United States,
> Appomattox Court House, Va., April 9, 1865.

General R. E. LEE,
Commanding C. S. Army.

GENERAL: In accordance with the substance of my letter to you of the 8th instant, I propose to receive the surrender of the Army of Northern Virginia on the following terms, to wit: Rolls of all the officers and men to be made in duplicate - one copy to be given to an officer to be designated by me, the other to be retained by such officer or officers as you may designate; the officers to give their individual paroles not to take up arms against the Government of the United States until properly exchanged, and each company or regimental commander to sign a like parole for the men of his command. The arms, artillery, and public property are to be parked and stacked, and turned over to the officers appointed by me to receive them. This will not embrace the side-arms of the officers, nor their private horses or baggage. This done, officers and men will be allowed to return to their homes, not to be disturbed by United States authority so long as they observe their paroles and the laws in force where they may reside.

Very respectfully,
U. S. GRANT,
Lieutenant-General.[276]

The original copy of this letter did not have the word "exchanged" after the word "properly" and Lee called it to Grant's attention. Lee said that with Grant's permission he would mark where the word should be inserted. He felt in his pocket for a pencil, according to Horace Porter, but could not find one. Porter said that he supplied the pencil which Lee used to make a caret in the letter. Porter retrieved the pencil and kept is as a souvenir of the occasion.[277]

Lee's heart was warmed by Grant's generosity in allowing the Confederate officers to retain their personal belongings. It was one of the few times during the interview when Grant was able to observe that Lee had any personal feelings about the surrender. Grant said:

When he read over the part of the terms about side-arms, horses, and private property of the officers, he remarked, with some feeling, I thought, that this would have a happy effect upon his army.[278]

Before a copy of Grant's letter was made in ink, Lee thought of his cavalrymen and artillerists who owned their own horses and decided that he would mention this to Grant in the hope that Grant might be willing to let them retain their animals. Horses would prove to be a very valuable asset to his men, most of whom lived on farms, and who would have to put in a crop after they returned home.

Lee told Grant that in the Confederate army the cavalrymen and artillerists owned their own horses and asked whether or not he was to understand that these men were to be permitted to retain them. Grant replied that as the terms were written they would not. Lee read over the terms a second time and remarked that it was clear that only officers' property had been mentioned in Grant's letter.[279]

Grant was willing to discuss the matter, however, and said that he knew most of the men were small farmers who would need their horses to put in a crop to carry themselves and their families through the next winter. Grant might have remembered his own days as a poor farmer. He said that he would not re-write his letter but would simply instruct his officers to let every man of the confederate army who claimed to own a horse or mule to take the animal home.[280] Lee again expressed his gratitude for this concession by saying that it would have a happy effect upon his men.

Horace Porter said that Grant first asked Colonel T. S. Bowers to make a copy of his letter in ink, but that Bowers was a little nervous, and the matter was turned over to E. S. Parker.[281] Grant might have wanted to give his honor to Bowers. Parker seems not to have mentioned this incident, because his biographer quoted it from Porter's account.[282]

Marshall said that he supplied Parker with some ink when the ink in the McLean inkstand proved unfit for use.[283] Marshall also said that he did not start to draft a reply to Grant's letter until Parker had finished making his copy of Grant's letter.[284]

While Marshall conversed with Sheridan, he said that Lee and Grant were talking with one another.[285] He implied that the conversation of the two generals was more or less private. He gave no indication that he knew Grant and Lee were talking about providing rations for the Confederate army until he heard Grant ask Sheridan how many rations he could provide.

G. H. Sharpe also said that the discussion between Grant and Lee on the subject of rations was private. He stated: "There was one moment when there was a whispered conversation between Grant and Lee which nobody in the room heard." He said that the officers learned about the subject of the whispered conversation only when Grant began to make arrangements for the distribution of rations to the Confederates.[286]

Porter indicated that he was able to hear everything that was said between the two generals.[287] This seems to be highly questionable, as are many other things reported by Porter.

Porter claimed that when the subject of providing rations came up, Grant asked Lee about how many men were in his force. Lee is said to have replied: "Indeed, I am not able to say."[288]

Grant himself said that he asked Lee about the number of his men, and that Lee answered, "About twenty-five thousand."[289]

Freeman was unwilling to accept the "literal accuracy" of Porter's version of this incident.[290] Grant's account should be preferred to that of Porter, especially in view of the testimony that much of the conversation on this subject was private.

Porter reported that some of Lee's comments indicated that he did not know that Sheridan had captured the Confederate supply trains at Appomattox Station on the night of April 8.[291] This seems very unlikely. Pendleton probably reported the presence and capture of the Confederate trains when he talked with Lee at 1 A.M. on April 9.[292]

George T. Peers, a resident of Appomatox Court House at the time of the surrender, said that the people in the village "heard early on Sunday Morning" that Sheridan had captured the Confederate provisions at Appomattox Station.[293] Since capture of the trains seems to have been common knowledge, Lee would most likely have known about it.

Porter said that Seth Williams tried to exchange some pleasantry with Lee, "as if he wanted to say something in a good-natured way to break up the frigidity of the conversation, but Lee was in no mood for pleasantries, and he did not unbend, or even relax the fixed sternness of his features."[294] His only response was supposed to have been a slight inclination of his head.

E. S. Parker did not think that Lee was the least bit aloof in talking to Seth Williams. "Lee was especially cordial to Seth Williams, who had been an adjutant under Lee when he was the commanding officer at West Point Academy."[295]

G. H. Sharpe said that Lee did respond to a pleasantry offered by someone in the room, although he did not say that it was Seth Williams who made the remark.

> Another, trying to relieve the awkwardness of the occasion, inquired: 'General Lee, what became of that white horse you rode in Mexico? He might not be dead yet; he was not so old?' General Lee bowed coldly, and replied: 'I left him at the White House on the Pamunky river, and have not seen him since.'[296]

One of Porter's suppositions was that Lee thought E. S. Parker, the Indian, was a member of the Negro race.[297] This was indignantly denied by Parker.[298] It seems that Porter's conjecture was without foundation in fact.

Another questionable matter is the report that Sheridan asked General Lee for permission to copy two dispatches he had sent Lee that day, protesting against alleged violations of the truce. Sheridan reported this incident and said that the protests were in regard to the withdrawal of the Confederate cavalry after the suspension of hostilities. Lee is said to have remarked, "I am sorry. It is probable that my cavalry at that point of the line did not fully understand the agreement."[299] There are no Confederate reports in regard to these dispatches, and there is no mention of them in the *Official Records.* Efforts to find Sheridan's Cavalry Headquarters records have been futile. Sheridan liked to write dispatches, and it is quite possible that he did send these dispatches to General Lee.

The accounts of the surrender conference vary in regard to the time when Grant introduced his officers to General Lee. Marshall[300] and Sheridan[301] stated that the introductions were made at the beginning of the conference. Grant[302] and Porter[303] said that they were made while the secretaries were making copies of the surrender letters. These accounts may not be as contradictory as they appear. Grant said that his generals were "severally presented" to General Lee while the surrender letters were being copied. There might have been a sort of group introduction at the very beginning, when Grant told Lee that the officers present were the members of his staff. Later on the men could have been presented individually.

Sheridan said that some of the officers entered the room at the beginning of the conference, were introduced to General Lee, and then withdrew until the surrender letters were being prepared.[304] Grant said that "a good portion" of his staff was present in the surrender room throughout the interview.[305] This statement indicates that not all the officers were present in the surrender room for the entire conference.

There is some confusion about which Union officers were actually present in the surrender room. George A. Forsyth tried to make a list of all those who were actually present in the room at any time during the conference. His list included the following: Grant, J. A. Rawlins, Seth Williams, Rufus Ingalls, Horace Porter, O. E. Babcock, P. H. Sheridan, M. R. Morgan, E. S. Parker, T. S. Bowers, Robert T. Lincoln, Adam Badeau, E. O. C. Ord, and Wesley Merritt.[306]

Wesley Merritt said: "I was not in the room, but once, on the suggestion of Colonel Babcock of Grant's staff, I went to the doorway and looked in, and saw the generals and their aides seated. The latter busily writing the others engaged in conversation."[307]

Should a man who went to the doorway one time and merely looked in the room be counted among those who were "actually present" in the room? This appears to be a matter of personal opinion. It is difficult to make any final judgment.

At least one other officer, in addition to the ones mentioned by Forsyth, claimed that he was in the room. He was George H. Sharpe. Sharpe made this very definite claim: "Gathered around the room were several officers, of whom I was one."[308] There can be no doubt that Sharpe thought he was present in the surrender room.

Forsyth indicated that Custer never entered the surrender room. He said that Custer and Merritt came up to the McLean House together but that only Merritt went inside while the conference was still in progress.[309]

Horace Porter indicated that Custer did enter the surrender room.

> There were present at McLean's house, besides Sheridan, Ord, Merritt, Custer, and the officers of Grant's staff, a number of other officers and one or two citizens who entered the room at different times during the interview.[310]

A. C. M. Pennington said that he and Custer were near the Northern Branch of the Appomattox River when General Lee rode to the McLean House for his conference with Grant. He said that he and Custer saw Lee as he rode to the McLean House and were still near the river when Lee came back.[311] If Pennington's testimony is regarded as trustworthy, it eliminates any possibility that Custer might have been in the surrender room during the surrender conference.

Sylvanus Cadwallader, Grant's favorite newspaper correspondent, said that he was in the surrender room and there seems to be no reason to doubt his claim.[312]

General Lee asked Colonel Marshall to draft a reply to Grant's letter. Marshall described the writing of this letter as follows:

> After a while Colonel Parker got through with his copy of General Grant's letter and I sat down to write a reply. I began it in the usual way: "I have the honor to acknowledge the receipt of your letter of such date," and then went on to say the terms were satisfactory. I took the letter over to General Lee, and read it, and said: "Don't say, 'I have the honor to acknowledge the receipt of your letter of such a date'; he is here; just say, 'I accept these terms.' "Then I wrote: -[313]
>
> The text of this letter was:
>
> Headquarters, Army of Northern Virginia
> April 9, 1865
>
> Lieut-Gen. U. S. Grant,
> Commanding Armies of the United States.
>
> General: I have received your letter of this date containing the terms of surrender of the Army of Northern Virginia as proposed by you. As they are substantially the same as those expressed in your letter of the 8th instant, they are accepted. I will proceed to designate the proper officers to carry the stipulations into effect.
>
> Very respectfully, your obedient servant,
> R. E. LEE,
> General.[314]

This letter had the heading:

"Headquarters of the Army of Northern Virginia
April 9, 1865"

It was the first time during the war that the headquarters of the Armies of the United States and the headquarters of the Army of Northern Virginia had been in the same room, at the same time.

Grant signed his letter and Lee signed his. Parker handed Grant's letter to Marshall and Marshall handed Parker Lee's reply. This simple exchange of letters marked the completion of the surrender and the virtual end of the Civil War. Marshall said:

> There was no theatrical display about it. It was in itself perhaps the greatest tragedy in the history of the world, but it was the simplest, plainest, and most thoroughly devoid of any attempt at effect, that you can imagine.[315]

Lee had mentioned to Grant that his army was starving, and Grant had promised to provide rations for the confederates. Lee had also talked about the need of forage for horses and mules. Grant had to tell Lee that the Union forces had no forage to spare, because they had been depending almost entirely on the country for that.[316]

During the brief conversation that followed the exchange of the surrender letters, Grant explained to Lee that he had come to the meeting as he was and without his sword, because he did not wish to detain Lee until he could send back to his wagons, which were several miles away. Marshall said: "This was the only reference made by any one to the subject of dress on that occasion."[317]

Horace Porter, on the other hand, reported a considerable conversation about swords. He said that Grant not only explained why he did not have on a sword, but that Lee said: "I am in the habit of wearing mine most of the time; I wear it invariably when I am among my troops, moving about through the army."[318]

This was another one of Porter's statements which had no foundation in fact. Freeman said: "There was, however, some misunderstanding here as Lee rarely wore a sword."[319]

Porter's description of the contrast in the appearance of Grant and Lee at the surrender conference has become so famous that many individuals imagine that it must have been on the mind of everyone who was present. It seems, however, that Grant never even thought of it while he was with Lee. He said: "In my rough travelingsuit, the uniform of a private with the straps of a lieutenant-general, I must have contrasted very strangely with a man so handsomely dressed, six feet high, and of faultless form. But this was not a matter that I thought of until afterward."[320]

With some minor exceptions, Porter's description of the dress of Grant and Lee seems to be fairly accurate. Porter said that Grant's blouse was unbuttoned.[321] G. H. Sharpe said that "one button of his coat - that is, the buttonhole was not where it should have been - it had clearly gone astray . . .".[322] Sharpe evidently meant to say that one of the buttons on Grant's coat was in the wrong buttonhole. If he was correct about this, it means that there was an even greater contrast between the appearance of Grant and Lee than was depicted by Porter.

A writer in *The Standard,* an English journal, once said:

> Only on one occasion does he (Lee) seem to have been accoutred with the slightest regard to military display or personal dignity; and that, characteristically, was the last occasion on which he wore the Confederate uniform - the occasion of his interview with General Grant on the 9th April, 1865.[323]

Before Grant and Lee parted, Lee asked that Meade be notified of the surrender, so that hostilities would not be resumed on his front. Grant agreed to send a message to Meade by two of his officers, who would ride through the Confederate lines, accompanied by a Confederate escort.[324] He also sent a dispatch to Meade saying that it was General Lee's desire for the members of the two armies to be kept separate, so that unpleasant personal encounters might be avoided.[325]

Horace Porter stated that Lee mentioned he had a thousand or more Union prisoners and would be glad to send them into the Union lines as soon as it could be arranged.[326] It seems likely that Lee would have mentioned this matter to Grant. He did have a considerable group of prisoners and was undoubtedly concerned about their welfare. Grant said that he told Lee that these men would be treated as paroled prisoners.[327]

Freeman thought that the surrender letters were exchanged to the front room of the McLean House at "about 3:45 P.M." on the afternoon of April 9.[328]

Perhaps Freeman based this conclusion on Porter's statement: "At a little before 4 o'clock General Lee shook hands with General Grant, bowed to the other officers, and with Colonel Marshall left the room."[329]

A careful examination of the evidence on this point raises serious questions about accepting 4 P.M. as the time when Lee left the McLean House and 3:45 P.M. as the time when the surrenders were exchanged.

Grant and Marshall did not state any definite time when Lee left the McLean House, although Marshall did say that "the whole course of the transaction . . . occupied perhaps an hour."[330] If Grant and Lee were together only about one hour, Lee left the McLean House between 2:30 and 3:00.

Morris Schaff thought it was between 2:30 and 3:00 when Lee left the McLean House. He said: "By this time the terms were copied, and, when they were signed, it was about half-past two or three o'clock. Lee shook hands with Grant, bowed to the other officers, and left the room."[331]

Sheridan stated that Lee left the McLean House about 3:00. He said: "About 3 o'clock in the afternoon the terms of surrender were written out and accepted, and General Lee left the house, as he departed cordially shaking hands with General Grant."[332]

E. P. Alexander wrote an account of the surrender in 1873. In that account he said that Lee returned "about 4 P.M." from his conference with Grant."[333] A good many years later, after he had re-examined all the evidence, Alexander changed this time and said: "I think it was after three o'clock when we saw Lee returning."[334]

It is known that the surrender was published to the Union troops at 4:00 P.M. Even the soldiers in the II and VI Union Army Corps, who were miles away from the McLean House, heard about the surrender at that hour. Meade said: "About 4 P.M. I received the welcome intelligence of the surrender of the Army of Northern Virginia."[335] Since it took considerable time for the news to travel that far, the event must have occurred somewhat earlier.

A member of the U. S. Signal Corps said that he heard the official news of the surrender at 3:00 P.M. He had established a station of observation on the Tibbs' house to watch for unauthorized withdrawals of the Confederate cavalry. He said: "The station was abandoned about 3 P.M., official news of the surrender of the Army of Northern Virginia having been received."[336] Since this man was stationed very close to the McLean House, it seems logical that he would have been among the first to hear the news.

Henderson and Company published a *Map of Appomattox Court House and Vicinity* in 1866. Under he heading "Historical Notes" it was said: "Generals Lee and Grant met at the home of Wilmer McLane, Esq., and after a brief interview, at 3½ o'clock P.M. on the 9th of April 1865, the articles of capitulation were signed by General Lee."

The many references to a time earlier than 4:00 or 3:45 as the time when the surrender letters were signed, form a body of testimony much too weighty to be disregarded. Further study should be made of this point.

Horace Porter portrayed Grant as leaving the McLean House just a few minutes after Lee. he said that Grant stepped down from the porch and saluted Lee by raising his hat.[337] This famous farewell in the yard of the McLean House has become so firmly planted in the minds of almost everyone that Freeman did not feel that it was necessary to document his description of it.[338]

This was not mentioned by Grant, Marshall, Sheridan, Sharpe, Badeau, Parker, Gibbon, Merritt, and Cadwallader. It was mentioned by George A. Forsyth,[339] who seems to have repeated many of Porter's errors. However, Forsyth did not say that Grant and Lee raised their hats to each other, as Porter did, but claimed that both generals simultaneously raised their hands in a military salute.

The chief objection to this event is that it portrays Grant as leaving the McLean House and riding to his headquarters immediately after he said farewell to Lee.

E. S. Parker implied that Grant did not leave the McLean House immediately after he told Lee good-bye. Parker said that after most of the other officers left the surrender room, he (Parker) remained in the room and wrote out the directions for carrying out the surrender terms. One was an order for the appointment of the three Union commissioners to help arrange the terms of the surrender. Another was a letter to Meade, ordering him to move his forces back to Burkeville. Although Parker claimed that he put these dispatches in his own words, the details in the order to Meade were far too important for Grant to leave them entirely in the hands of his military secretary. The letter to Meade was as follows:

HEADQUARTERS, ARMIES OF THE UNITED STATES,
APPOMATTOX COURT HOUSE, April 9, 1865.

General Meade:

General: The Fifth Corps of the Army of the Potomac and the Twenty-Fourth Corps of the Army of the James will remain here until the stipulations of the surrender of the C. S. Army, known as the Army of Northern Virginia, entered into by General R. E. Lee and the lieutenant-general commanding, have been carried into effect, and the captured and surrendered public property has been secured. All the other forces will be moved back to Burkeville, starting tomorrow where they will go into camp. The chief ordnance officer of the Army of the Potomac will collect and take charge of all captured and surrendered ordnance and ordnance stores and remove them to Burkeville. The acting chief quartermaster of the Army of the James will collect and take charge of all the captured and surrendered quartermaster's property and store and remove them to Burkeville. You will please give such orders to your troops and officers of the staff departments as will secure the execution of the foregoing instructions. The troops going to Burkeville will turn over to those remaining here all the subsistence stores -they may have a bare sufficiency to take them back.

By command of Lieutenant-General Grant.
E. S. PARKER,
Acting Assistant Adjutant-General.[340]

As suggested above, it seems logical that Grant would have waited to see the final copy of such an important letter before sending it to Meade, since it involved the movement of many thousands of men.

Another reason for believing that Grant did not leave the McLean House along with Lee is a conversation which Henry Heth claimed to have had with Grant on the "day of the surrender." Heth did not say that he talked to Grant in the McLean House but he did say that it was in a room. Since Grant did not enter any other house at Appomattox Court House except the McLean House, the conversation must have been held there. It is said to have lasted for thirty minutes. The thirty minutes could have been sometime between 3 and 4 o'clock on the afternoon of April 9, based on the presumption that Lee left about 3 o'clock, and that Grant was waiting on Parker to make copies of important military dispatches.

Heth's account of his conversation with Grant is as follows:

> The day of the surrender I went to General Grant's headquarters on some business. General Grant shook me by the hand most cordially and said, "Come into this room; I want to talk to you." We took seats. Grant asked, "Heth, do you remember when we were last together?" "In St. Louis, I believe in 1852." The General said, "Yes, and do you remember how near I came to breaking my neck and yours?" "Yes; it would have made little difference, as far as history is concerned, if you had broken my neck, and now, as our troubles are at an end, I am glad that you got through safely; but, Grant, during the past three years I have wished a thousand times you had broken your neck when you ran into that cow." Grant laughed and said, "We went to Jefferson Barracks, did we not?" I replied, "We did." . . . We chatted for half an hour about old times . . . but our war was not once referred to . . . . "We have been chatting here for half an hour, and you have not asked me once to take a drink. I have not had one for three months." He laughed and said, "I have nothing here to drink, but if you will send your orderly with mine, you will find something to drink at your quarters when you reach them." On my return I found two gallons of good whiskey in my ambulance.[341]

Grant's reluctance to discuss the war sounds authentic, because he did not even mention the surrender to General Lee until Lee brought it up. His statement that he did not have any whiskey seems to fit the McLean House, as there is no evidence that there was any whiskey there at the time of the surrender.

No evidence has been found to substantiate Heth's claim that he had this conversation with Grant. Heth said that it took place on the day of the surrender, and it seems that it must have been then or not at all, because Grant hardly had time for such a long conversation on April 10. No final judgment seems possible at this time.

G. H. Sharpe said that as soon as Lee left the McLean House Grant called his officers together and appointed different ones to go to the V and XXIV Corps and "ask every man who has three rations to turn over two of them. . . . General Lee's army is on the verge of starvation!"[342]

Some weight is given to Sharpe's testimony by the account of a member of the 118th Pennsylvania Regiment. He said that "the soldiers of Bartlett's division shared their provender with their fallen foemen until every haversack was empty. The sweet aroma of real coffee staggered the Confederates, condensed milk and sugar appalled them, and they stood aghast at just a little butter which one soldier, more provident than his fellows, happened to have preserved."[343]

Since it is quite clear that Grant had a number of very important matters which demanded his attention immediately after the close of the surrender conference, it seems reasonable to believe that he remained at the McLean House long enough to complete the preparation of important military dispatches, such as the letter to Meade. He might have left the McLean House about 4:15 P.M., because it is known that he stopped along the road, between the McLean House and his headquarters, at 4:30 P.M., to send the news of the surrender to E. M. Stanton, the Secretary of War, in Washington.

GENERAL LEE LEAVES THE McLEAN HOUSE

General Lee and Colonel Marshall, with Sergeant Tucker, rode away slowly from the McLean House. Word seems to have reached the Confederate lines that they were coming, because E. P. Alexander ordered his cannoneers to form in line along the road and uncover in silence as Lee rode by. Alexander wrote several accounts of what happened, and his earliest version, in some respects at least, seems to be the best.

> The universal desire to express to him the unabated love and confidence of the army had led to the formation of the gunners of a few battalions of artillery along the roadside, with orders to take off their hats in silence as he rode by. When he approached, however, the men could not be restrained, but burst into the wildest cheering, which the adjoining infantry lines took up, and breaking ranks, they all crowded around him cheering at the tops of their voices. Gen. Lee stopped his horse, and after

> gaining silence, made the only speech to his men that he ever made. He was very brief, and gave no excuses or apologies for his surrender, but said he had done all in his power for his men, and urged them to go as quickly and quietly to their homes as possible, to resume peaceful avocations, and to be good citizens as they had been soldiers; and this advice marked the course which he himself pursued so faithfully to the end.[344]

Later on, Alexander discovered that he was mistaken in saying that Lee's speech at Appomattox was the only one he ever made to his troops. There was another occasion, it seems, but hardly more than one, when Lee had spoken to his men.[345]

There are various versions of what General Lee actually said to his troops. In addition to the statements mentioned by Alexander, some said that he told his men they would be paroled. F. M. Colston claimed that he was close enough to catch some but not all of Lee's words.

> He stopped his horse, and, looking around, said: "Men, we have fought the war together and I have done the best I could for you. You will all be paroled and go to your homes until exchanged." I was close to him and climbed upon a wagon-hub to see and hear distinctly. He said a few more words which I cannot repeat accurately, but those which I record are engraved upon my memory.[346]

All seem to agree that Lee spoke very briefly, not more than a few sentences. He probably spoke quietly and deliberately in a voice that did not carry very far; many were able to catch only a few snatches of what he said. It is believed that the reports by Alexander and Colston are reasonably accurate.

Foreign writers were greatly impressed by the treatment which Lee received at this time from his troops. Sir Frederick Maurice said:

> The reception of the Confederate Commander-in-Chief by his men, when he returned after his interview with Grant to tell them of the surrender, is, I think, more remarkable than is the story of any ovation accorded by his troops to a conqueror.[347]

The air was charged with emotion as Lee spoke to his old campaigners, men who had trudged on through the rain and mud to Appomattox Court House largely because of their loyalty to Lee, rather than because of their devotion to the Confederacy. There was not a dry eye among them, as they crowded around to try to shake his hand or touch his horse. Some appealed to him to get them exchanged and try to continue the struggle, but he made no reply to such suggestions.[348] He knew the war was over.

By Timothy O'Sullivan

McLean's House, Appomattox Court House, Virginia, April 1865

(From Contemporary Lithograph)

Lee and Grant Meeting on April 9

By. J. R. Chapin

The Formal Surrender of the Army of Northern Virginia on April 12

(From Contemporary Lithograph)

General Lee's Last Council of War

One of the best descriptions of the feeling of Lee's troops was written by Francis Lawley for *The Fortnightly Review:*

> As the great Confederate captain rode back from his interview with General Grant, the news of the surrender acquired shape and consistency, and could no longer be denied. The effect on the worn and battered troops - some of whom had fought since April, 1861, and (sparse survivors of hecatombs of fallen comrades) had passed unscratched through such hurricanes of shot as within four years no other men had ever experienced — passes mortal description. Whole lines of battle rushed up to their beloved old chief, and choking with emotion, broke ranks and struggled with each other to wring him once more by the hand. Men who had fought through the war, and knew what the agony and humility of that moment must be to him, strove with a refinement of unselfishness and tenderness which he alone could fully appreciate, to lighten his burden and nitigate his pain. With tears pouring down both cheeks, General Lee at length commanded voice enough to say, "Men we have fought the war together. I have done the best that I could for you." Not an eye that looked on that scene was dry. Nor was this the emotion of sickly sentimentalists, but of rough and rugged men familiar with hardship, danger, and death in a thousand shapes, mastered by sympathy and feeling for another which they had never experienced on their own account. I know of no other passage of military history so touching unless, in spite of the melodramatic colouring which French historians have loved to shed over the scene, it can be found in the *Adiuex de Fontainebleau.*[349]

Alexander said that when Lee returned from the Court House that he informed the "principal officers" of the terms of the surrender.[350] This was probably the time when Lee informed Longstreet, Gordon, and Pendleton that they would serve as the Confederate commissioners to help arrange the formal terms of surrender.

Alexander said that Lee spoke to him about Grant's willingness to let the Confederate soldiers keep their privately owned horses and that this seemed to be a point of special gratification to him.[351]

According to Colonel W. W. Blackford, there was considerable activity around the apple tree when Lee came back from his conference with Grant. One of the principal items which demanded attention was the feeding of the Confederates by the Union commissary, and this required the presence of a number of Union officers from time to time. There were some who apparently came more out of curiosity to see General Lee than to transact business. Colonels Taylor and Venable received the visitors and conducted them to General Lee, who greeted them with a military salute. Most of the interviews were short, for General Lee was not in a mood to exchange pleasantries. The net result of these interviews was that rations were soon issued to thousands of hungry Confederates, many of whom had lived on parched corn during most of the retreat from Petersburg.[352]

About sundown, General Lee rode from the apple tree to his headquarters, a mile or so away on the Richmond-Lynchburg Stage Road, and again there was a tremendous outburst of emotion among his troops.

> As soon as he entered this avenue of these old soldiers, the flower of the army, the men who had stood to their duty through thick and thin in so many battles, wild, heartfelt cheers arose which so touched General Lee that tears filled his eyes and trickled down his cheeks as he rode his splendid charger, hat in hand, bowing his acknowledgements.
>
> This exhibition of feeling on his part found quick response from the men whose cheers changed to choking sobs, as with streaming eyes and many evidences of affection they waved their hats as he passed. Each group began in the same way, with cheers, and ended in the same way, with sobs, all along the route to his quarters. Grim bearded men threw themselves on the ground, covered their faces with their hands and wept like children. Officers of all ranks made no attempt to conceal their feelings, but sat on their horses and cried aloud, and among these I remember seeing General W. H. F. Lee, General R. E. Lee's son, much moved.[353]

SENDING NEWS OF THE SURRENDER TO WASHINGTON

Grant did not think of sending a message to Washington about the surrender until he left the McLean House and was on his way back to his headquarters. Dismounting by the side of the road, he sat on a stone and called for paper and pencil. Adam Badeau offered his order book, and Grant wrote out the following message to E. M. Stanton, Secretary of War:

> General Lee surrendered the army of Northern Virginia this afternoon on terms proposed by myself. The accompanying additional correspondence will show the conditions fully.[354]

The message was dated at 4:30 P.M., April 9, 1865.

A telegraph wire had not yet been extended to Appomattox Court House, so it was necessary to send the dispatch from Appomattox Station. William R. Plum gave the following account of how the surrender telegram was sent:

> Laverty and Schermorhorn were called to General Grant's presence and the foregoing message and others were given them with directions to find the wire. They soon lost the way but quickly righting their error they reached Appomattox station to which point the wire was already repaired, and selected for their office a box car laden with bags of sand intended for defensive purposes. As soon as a ground wire was laid the operators called Petersburg office. The operator on duty there was prompt to reply. After telling the glorious news, Petersburg connected the War Department direct. Congratulatory replies from the President and Secretary of War were received at near five o'clock. So quickly was this good work accomplished, that Grant was both surprised and pleased. Within two hours after the surrender, the line was extended to Grant's at Appomattox Court House. The intoxicating news spread like lightning rapidity all over the land. Bells were rung, cannon fired, rockets sent up, bonfires built and meetings held. From that box-car at the station in the midst of the armies, had been forwarded the few words that made tears of joy gather in the eye of millions, who now saw the clouds break entirely away, leaving a clear sky for the great future.[355]

It does not seem that this enthusiastic account by William R. Plum can be accepted without some reservations. Grant's dispatch was not written until 4:30 P.M. The message had to be carried to Appomattox Station before it could be sent off, and the telegraph operators lost their way temporarily while going from the Court House to the Station. The message had to be relayed through Petersburg. All this supposedly took place within half an hour, and congratulatory replies were received from President Lincoln and Secretary Stanton about five o'clock!

There are several reports in the *Official Records* which make this appear to be highly questionable.

In a message to Major General Dix of New York, Edwin M. Stanton, Lincoln's Secretary of War, indicated that he did not hear of the surrender until about 9:00 P.M. His message, dated April 9 at 9 P.M., said:

> This Department has just received official report of the surrender, this day, of General Lee and his army to Lieutenant-General Grant, on the terms proposed by Grant.[356]

Stanton did not send a message of congratulations to Grant until 9:30 P.M. He said:

> Thanks be to Almighty God for the great victory with which he has this day crowned you and the gallant army under your com-

mand. The thanks of this Department and of the Government, and of the people of the United States, their reverence and honor, have been deserved and will be rendered to you and the brave and gallant officers and soldiers of your army for all time.[357]

Stanton did not send out an order requiring a salute of 200 guns to be fired until 10 P.M. on April 9.

WAR DEPARTMENT,
Washington, D.C., April 9, 1865 — 10 P.M.

Ordered, That a salute of 200 guns be fired at the headquarters of every army and department, and at every post and arsenal in the United States, and at the Military Academy at West Point on the day of the receipt of this order, R. E. Lee and the Army of Northern Virginia to Lieutenant-General Grant and the army under his command. Report of the receipt and execution of this order to be made to the Adjutant General, Washington.

EDWIN M. STANTON.

(Copy to governors of States, mayors of principal cities, commanding generals of military departments, and others.)[358]

Philip Van Doren Stern said: "Word from Appomattox reached Washington so late on Sunday night that only a few newspaper men were on hand to hear the news of victory. . . . The rollicking correspondents sent out telegrams from Maine to California and then proceeded to get grandly and gloriously drunk."[359]

It is known that news of the surrender did not reach Philadelphia until 9:30 on Sunday evening.[360] This is in line with Stanton's message saying that he heard the news about 9:00 P.M.

The news evidently spread with something less than the "lightning rapidity" mentioned by Plum.

GRANT RETURNS TO HIS HEADQUARTERS

Horace Porter stated that Grant was reluctant to discuss the surrender after he went to his headquarters, and that he waited until after supper to say that he believed Lee's surrender would lead to the cessation of fighting on all fronts.[361]

Grant always seems to have been reluctant to discuss the surrender. It is said that Grant's wife "took note of the fact that in after years he never discussed the surrender with his family."[362]

Porter did not indicate that Grant discussed any other important matters after he returned to his headquarters beyond making the simple announcement that he intended to start his return to Washington on the next day.

Henry Heth said that one of his requests on April 9 was answered in a very generous manner, and that he always thought that Grant was really responsible for it. Heth stated:

> On one of my marches in 1864 I saw on the roadside the running gear of an abandoned one-horse vehicle. I directed one of my couriers to remain with this relic and attach it to my headquarters' wagon and bring it to camp. I had the wagon repaired, a body made for it, and at my own expense. I considered this wagon as my private property. I wrote a note to General Seth Williams, General Grant's Adjutant General, and asked whether or not I would be permitted to take my effects home in this wagon. He replied that my note had been referred to the commanding general, who decided that I could not have the wagon. Not in a very good humor, I lay down in my ambulance to take a nap. I had not slept for three nights. I was about falling asleep when I heard the rattling of sabres outside and my name called. I arose and recognized Seth Williams and Rufus Ingalls, chief quartermaster of Grant's army. General Williams said, pointing to the small wagon, "Heth, is that the thing you have been writing about?" "Yes," I said, "and I hope it will be as useful to your army as it has been to me." He replied, "Old fellow, I had to answer your note as I did. The General thought it might establish a bad precedent. Have you any good ambulances in your division?" I said, "Yes." "Any good mules?" I said I had some splendid mules. Williams said, "Take the best ambulance, and hitch to it four of the best mules you have and go home in style." Turning to General Ingalls, he said, "That will be all right, Rufus, will it not?" General Ingalls replied, "Yes, take a half a dozen if you wish." I was not slow in availing myself of this permission and I have always thought that General Grant sent Seth Williams and Rufus Ingalls, both of whom were old friends, on this errand. I did not take six, but did take one, and four splendid mules, which, on arriving at my home, I turned over to my father-in-law, and it enabled him to make a crop that year.[363]

Heth's request for this wagon might have given Grant the idea to issue an order to Gibbon directing that the Confederate wagons at Appomattox Court House be left for the country people to pick up.[364]

FORMAL TERMS OF SURRENDER

Three Union commissioners and three Confederate commissioners were appointed by Grant and Lee respectively to draw up the formal terms of surrender for the Army of Northern Virginia.

Grant appointed Major General John Gibbon, Brevet Major General Charles Griffin, and Brevet Major General Wesley Merritt to serve as the Union commissioners. Grant's order was as follows:

SPECIAL ORDERS. HDQRS. ARMIES OF THE UNITED STATES,
in the Field, April 9, 1865.

Maj. Gen. John Gibbon, Bvt. Maj. Gen. Charles Griffin, and Bvt. Maj. Gen. Wesley Merritt are hereby designated to carry into effect the stipulations of this day entered into between General R. E. Lee, commanding C. S. armies, and Lieutenant-General Grant, commanding Armies of the United States, in which General Lee surrenders to General Grant the Army of Northern Virginia.

Bvt. Brig. Gen. George H. Sharpe, assistant provost-marshall-general, will receive and take charge of rolls called for by the above-mentioned stipulations.

By command of Lieutenant-General Grant:
E. S. PARKER,
Lieutenant-Colonel and Acting Assistant Adjutant-General.[365]

Lee appointed Lieutenant General J. Longstreet, Major General J. B. Gordon, and Brigadier General W. N. Pendleton to serve as the Confederate commissioners. Lee's order was as follows:

SPECIAL ORDERS,) HDQRS. ARMIES OF THE CONFED. STATES,
No. - . April 9, 1865.

Lieut. Gen. J. Longstreet, Maj. Gen. J. B. Gordon, and Brig. Gen. W. N. Pendleton are hereby designated to carry into effect the stipulations this day entered into between Lieut. Gen. U. S. Grant, commanding Armies of the United States, and General R. E. Lee, commanding armies of the Confederate States, in which General Lee surrendered to General Grant the Army of Northern Virginia.

By command of General R. E. Lee:
W. H. TAYLOR,
Lieutenant-Colonel and Assistant Adjutant-General.[366]

The evidence indicates that Grant appointed the Union commissioners before he left the McLean House. Ely Parker said that he remained in the surrender room and wrote out the order in accordance with Grant's wishes.[367]

Marshall indicated that Lee appointed his commissioners very soon after the conclusion of the surrender conference.

After having this general conversation we took leave of

General Grant, and went off to appoint commissioners to attend to the details of the surrender.[368]

The terms as agreed upon by the Union and Confederate commissioners were as follows:

APPOMATTOX COURT-HOUSE, VA., April 10, 1865.

Agreement entered into this day in regard to the surrender of the Army of Northern Virginia to the United States authorities.

1st. The troops shall march by brigades and detachments to a designated point, stack their arms, deposit their flags, sabers, pistols, &c., and from thence march to their homes under charge of their officers, superintended by their respective division and corps commanders, officers retaining their side arms, and the authorized number of private horses.

2d. All public horses and public property of all kinds to be turned over to staff officers designated by the United States authorities.

3d. Such transportation as may be agreed upon as necessary for the transportation of the private baggage of officers will be turned over at the end of the trip to the nearest U. S. quartermasters, receipts being taken for the same.

4th. Couriers and mounted men of the artillery and cavalry, whose horses are their own private property, will be allowed to retain them.

5th. The surrender of the Army of Northern Virginia shall be construed to include all the forces operating with that army on the 8th instant, the date of commencement of negotiations for surrender, except such bodies of cavalry as actually made their escape previous to the surrender, and except also such pieces of artillery as were more than twenty miles from Appomattox Court House at the time of surrender on the 9th instant.

JOHN GIBBON,
Major-General of Volunteers.
CHAS. GRIFFIN
Brevet Major-General, U. S. Volunteers.
W. MERRITT,
Brevet Major-General.
J. LONGSTREET,
Lieutenant-General.
J. B. GORDON,
Major-General.
W. N. PENDLETON,
Brigadier-General and Chief of Artillery.[369]

John Gibbon wrote the following account of the way the six commissioners went about their work:

> The six officers appointed to arrange the details of the surrender met in a room of the hotel of the town; but this was a bare and cheerless place, and at my suggestion we adjourned to the room in the McLean House where Grant and Lee had held their conference. Here we at once organized and began to discuss the subject before us, and after talking for a while it was suggested that I should write out the several propositions covering the surrender. This I did in pretty much the same shape as that finally adopted. When I came to the fifth clause I paused, for there was an important question involved: Who should be considered as included in the surrender? It was kwown that a part of the cavalry had made its escape toward Lynchburg just about the time the surrender took place. The matter was discussed for a few minutes, when General Gordon rose to his feet and made quite a speech, during which he said that, as they had been treated with so much liberality, he felt disposed, so far as he was concerned, to act liberally also, and that he considered his *personal honor* (with emphasis) required him to give the most liberal interpretation to every question which came up for decision. Longstreet sat still and said nothing, but when Gordon sat down he remarked very quietly that he proposed the surrender should include all troops belonging to the army, except such cavalry as actually made its escape, and any artillery that was beyond twenty miles from Appomattox Court House at the time of the surrender. This proposition was at once accepted by unanimous consent, and the terms as agreed to were duly drawn up and signed that night.
>
> Mindful of the prize I had seen Custer carrying off, and having no surplus twenty-five dollar gold pieces to pay out, it occurred to me to secure a cheaper table. I therefore directed that the old pine camp-table which I had used all through the war be placed in the room. This was covered with a blanket, and when, at 8:30 P.M., the members assembled to sign the final agreement, they signed on this table. Triplicate copies were signed, one being retained by the officers of each army. The third copy I kept, and afterward presented to the Historical Society of Maryland, in the rooms of which, in the city of Baltimore, it is now preserved.[370]

Gibbon also said that the next day he placed his table in the hands of one of the clerks at his corps headquarters, and this man smoothed and sandpapered the top and placed on it the following inscription:

ON THIS TABLE

> was signed the Final Agreement for the surrender of the "Army of Northern Virginia," at Appomattox C. H., Va., 8:30 P.M. April 10th 1865 by Lt. Gen. J. Longstreet, Maj. Gen. J. B. Gordon and Brig. Gen. W. N. Pendleton, C.S.A., and Maj. Gen. John Gibbon, Bvt. Maj. Gen'l. Charles Griffin and Brev. Maj. Gen. W. Merritt, U. S. Army.[371]

As Gibbon indicated, the main point discussed by the commissioners was Point Five of the surrender terms. All the other points, it seems, were apparently formulated in accordance with the directions of Grant, which he stated at his conference with Lee on the morning of April 10 or to his commissioners at some other time.

It is known that Grant insisted that the final act of the surrender should be rather formal, instead of letting the Confederates merely throw down their arms where they were and walk away. J. L. Chamberlain said that he was informed by Griffin that the Confederates had begged hard to be allowed to stack their arms on the ground where they were, and let us go and pick them up after they had gone; but that Grant did not think this quite respectful enough to anybody, including the United States of America; and while he would have all private property respected, and would permit officers to retain their side arms, he insisted that the surrendering army as such should march out in due order, and lay down all tokens of Confederate authority and organized hostility to the United States, in immediate presence of some representative portion of the Union army.[372]

The account written by John Gibbon seems to imply that the commissioners were not able to complete their work until sometime after dark on April 10. Gibbon stated that "the terms as agreed to were duly drawn up and signed that night." Unfortunately, he did not give any details about the signing, which took place at 8:30 P.M. He said that the "members assembled to sign the final agreement" on Gibbon's table and that triplicate copies were signed. This indicates that there was some formality about the ceremony of signing these papers. It seems reasonable to believe that others might have been present in addition to the six generals who actually signed the documents.

The generals signed in the order indicated by their rank, with the Union generals being the first to sign.

A copy of the surrender agreement was probably dispatched to Grant at Prospect Station very soon after it had been signed. An exchange of notes between Stanton and Grant on April 10 implies that Grant knew about the provisions of Point Five within half an hour after the papers were signed.

On the afternoon of April 10, Edwin M. Stanton, Secretary of War, sent Grant an inquiry about the status of Rosser's men and some of the other troops generally considered a part of the Army of Northern Virginia.

WAR DEPARTMENT,
Washington City, April 10, 1865, — 3:50 P.M.

Lieutenant-General GRANT:

Rosser and the troops operating about Loudon form part of the Army of Northern Virginia reporting to Lee. Are they included in the surrender, or only those under Lee's immediate personal command? The troops in Western Virginia have also gone as part of the Army of Northern Virginia.

EDWIN M. STANTON,
Secretary of War.[373]

While the exact time when Grant received this inquiry is not known, the lateness of his answer indicates that he evidently waited until the commissioners had completed their work before he sent a reply.

PROSPECT STATION, April 10, 1865-
9:05 P.M.

Honorable E. M. STANTON,
Secretary of War, Washington, D.C.:

The surrender was only of the men left with the pursued army at the time of surrender. All prisoners captured in battle previous to the surrender stand same as other prisoners of war, and those who had escaped and were detached at the time are not included. I think, however, there will be no difficulty now in bringing in on the terms voluntarily given to General Lee all the fragments of the Army of Northern Virginia, and it may be the army under Johnston also. I wish Hancock would try it with Mosby.

U. S. GRANT,
Lieutenant-General.[374]

CONFERENCE BETWEEN GRANT AND LEE ON APRIL 10

A second conference between Grant and Lee was held on the morning of April 10. The place was a little knoll, just east of the Court House, and not far from the Richmond-Lynchburg Stage Road. It was between the picket lines of the two armies.

The conference was initiated by Grant. He said:

I determined to return to Washington at once, with a view to putting a stop to the purchase of supplies, and what I now deemed other useless outlay of money. Before leaving,

> however, I thought I would like to see General Lee again; so next morning I rode out beyond our lines toward his headquarters, preceded by a bugler and a staff-officer carrying a white flag.[375]

What was the weather like during this open-air conference? Grant made no comment on the weather. Colonel Charles Marshall said that it was raining.[376] Sylvanus Cadwallader said that drizzling rain set in about the time the conference started.[377] Adam Badeau stated that the conference was held under a bright spring sun,[378] and Ely Parker said that the sun came up from behind Grant and Lee and made a very pretty sight.[379]

Freeman thought that "rain was falling steadily" on the morning of April 10, 1865.[380]

Since some say that the sun was shining, while others say that it was drizzling rain or raining, it seems likely that a light rain or intermittent showers prevailed during the morning of the 10th. It does not appear reasonable that Grant would have tried to hold a conference with Lee in the midst of a steady downpour.

Parker,[381] Badeau,[382] and Porter[383] said that Grant rode out to meet Lee about 9 o'clock in the morning. It took some little time to get in touch with Lee, and it seems that the conference did not actually get underway until about 10 o'clock. Sylvanus Cadwallader was very definite about the time when the conference began. He stated that the time was "ten o'clock A.M., Monday, April 10, 1865."[384]

10 o'clock was the time accepted by Freeman for the beginning of the conference.[385] This appears to be the correct time.

A controversial point about this conference is the manner in which General Lee approached the place where it was held.

Grant apparently had not notified General Lee that he wanted to have a conference on the morning of the 10th.[386] He and a large group of his officers simply rode out toward the Confederate lines in the direction of Lee's headquarters. When they approaced the Confederate pickets, they were halted until General Lee could be notified that Grant desired to have a conference with him. As soon as Lee was informed about Grant's presence, he promptly rode out to meet him, accompanied by a single orderly.

Horace Porter said that Lee "rode at a gallop" to receive Grant.[387] This statement was repeated by Freeman.[388]

Sylvanus Cadwallader said that "Lee, accompanied by an orderly came galloping up the slope."[389]

This was disputed by some of the Confederates who were on the picket line on the morning of April 10. Sergeant John Thomas Gibson of the First Regiment of Engineer Troops wrote to General Jubal A. Early on January 24, 1888, to deny the truth of Porter's statement. He said:

> My object in this is to deny the statement of General Porter in the particular referred to and to testify to the dignity and grandeur and gravity of Gen. Lee which never forsook him; but which on this occasion was particularly striking and marked with a solemnity befitting the occasion and to be appreciated only by his faithful soldiers who witnessed the going down of the Southern Conference never to rise again. Lee showed no haste, no hurry and no relaxation of his great and wonted dignity on this occasion. As he passed by us to the top of the hill we remarked how stately, grand and solemn he was, going alone with his orderly to hold a brief interview with the general who had overpowered him and his army.[390]

Gibson's testimony seems to be an eye-witness account of what actually happened. He commented only on what he saw and said that he considered Porter's other statements to be fair and free from prejudice. Since his object was to deny Porter's statement that General Lee rode at a gallop to his conference with Grant, it is impossible to reconcile the two versions of this matter.

Reports in regard to the conversation between Grant and Lee vary a great deal. In this instance, there is a rather full statement from Grant, and it is believed that his statement should take precedence over all other statements.

> Lee soon mounted his horse, seeing who it was, and met me. We had there between the lines, sitting on horseback, a very pleasant conversation of over half an hour, in the course of which Lee said to me that the South was a big country, and that we might have to march over it three or four times before the war entirely ended, but that now we would be able to do it, as they could no longer resist us. He expressed it as his earnest hope, however, that we would not be called upon to cause more loss and sacrifice of life; but he could not foretell the result. I then suggested to General Lee that there was not a man in the Confederacy whose influence with the soldiery and the whole people was as great as his, and that if he would now advise the surrender of all the armies I had no doubt his advice would be followed with alacrity. But Lee said that he could not do that without consulting the President first. I knew there was no use to urge him to do anything against his ideas of what was right.[391]

During their exchange of letters prior to the surrender, Lee had insisted that he wanted to talk to Grant about the restoration of peace, rather than limit their discussion to the surrender of the Army of Northern Virginia. Since the Federal authorities had previously forbidden Grant to meet Lee for a discussion of peace, he wrote Lee that he had no authority to treat on the subject of peace. At their conference on April 10, however, Grant tried to persuade Lee to use his influence to bring about a general peace by advising the surrender of all the Confederate armies. With almost a touch of grim humor, Lee replied that he could not follow Grant's suggestion without first consulting President Davis. Lee evidently did not display any unpleasant feeling about the matter, because Grant said that he thought they had "a very pleasant conversation."

In Sylvanus Cadwallader's version of this conversation, it is alleged that Lee actually reminded Grant that he had previously turned down an opportunity to talk about arranging a general peace. "During this conference Lee stated that if Grant had assented to a meeting which he had proposed some weeks before, peace would undoubtedly have resulted therefrom."[392]

If Lee did not actually make this statement, it is certainly reasonable to presume that such a thought went through his mind. However, in fairness to Grant, it should be pointed out that he undoubtedly would have consented to discuss peace with Lee at an earlier meeting if he had received permission to do so from the Federal authorities.

C. A. Dana, evidently quoting Grant, said that Lee told Grant that "he had always been for the Union in his heart and could find no justification for the politicians who had brought on the war, whose origin he had believed to have been in the folly of the extremists on both sides."[393]

Horace Porter's account of the conversation between Grant and Lee on the morning of April 10 was based on what he remembered from the outline which Grant gave to his staff on the evening after the interview. It includes several statements which Grant did not mention in his account, but Grant's account is preferred because it is first-hand, while Porter's is second-hand. The comment which Freeman made about Porter's narrative appears to be entirely justified. He said that "it seems a bit embroidered with time, and it has the emphasis in the wrong place."[394]

Colonel Charles Marshall stated that General Lee told him that Grant wanted him (Lee) to go to see President Lincoln in the interest of peace.[395] Horace Porter said that he asked Grant about this and that Grant's recollection was distinct that he had made no such suggestion.[396] It appears that Marshall was mistaken about this, as well as being mistaken in thinking that Grant and Lee might have had their conference on April 10 at the famous apple tree.[397]

Near the end of the conference, Sheridan rode up and asked permission to cross the lines and visit some of his old friends in the Confederate army. Permission was granted and Sheridan, Rufus Ingalls, and Seth Williams set out to find their acquaintances.[398]

Before the conference concluded, Gibbon said that Grant beckoned him forward and said: "General Lee is desirous that his officers and men should have on their persons some evidence that they are paroled prisoners, so that they will not be disturbed." General Lee then remarked that he desired simply to do whatever was in his power to protect his men from anything disagreeable. Gibbon stated that he thought that could be arranged, as he had a small printing press on which blank forms could be printed, and these could be filled out and one given to each officer and man, signed by their own officers and distributed as required. General Lee thought that this would be a very agreeable arrangement.[399]

Sometime before the surrender was completed, Gibbon said that he saw General Lee again and that the Confederate leader then expressed some apprehension about this arrangement, because he thought that the United States authorities probably would not respect the signature of his officers, and that the paroles ought to be signed by Union officers. Gibbon said that Longstreet happened to be present and that they both pointed out to General Lee that it would be impractical to have Union officers sign the paroles because of the lack of time. General Lee finally said that he would leave the whole matter in the hands of Longstreet, which meant, in effect, that the decision to let Confederate officers sign the paroles would be carried out.[400]

Another matter which seems to have come up for discussion at the conference on the morning of April 10 was the subject of allowing Confederate couriers, artillerymen, and cavalrymen, who owned their own horses, to be allowed to retain them. Gibbon said that General Lee turned to General Grant and said: "General, you have excepted private horses from the surrender. Now most of my couriers and many of the artillery and cavalry own their own horses. How will it be about them?"

General Grant replied at once, speaking to me: "They will be allowed to retain them." Turning to General Lee, he added: "They will need them in putting in their spring crops."[401]

Some have thought that Gibbon confused the conversation on April 9 with the conversation on April 10, but it seems that he was correct in saying that Lee brought up the matter again at the conference on the 10th because Gibbon's report in regard to the language which Lee used about the horses on the 10th is virtually the same as that which was used about the horses in the formal terms of surrender.

Gibbon stated that all of the Union commissioners (Gibbon, Griffin, and Merritt) were at the conference on the 10th, and that they, accompanied by a number of other officers, rode through the picket-line to Longstreet's headquarters, escorted by a member of his staff.[402] The presence of Merritt is verified by a message from Gibbon to Merritt in the *Official Records,* asking Merritt to come to the conference.[403]

Another item which might have been discussed by Grant and Lee was the matter of allowing paroled Confederates to pass through Federal lines and travel free on government transports and military railroads in order to reach their homes. Although it is somewhat garbled, the account in Parker's biography indicates that this matter came up at the conference.[404]

The order in regard to Confederates needing assistance on their way home was as follows:

Special Orders,
No. 73.

HEADQUARTERS, ARMIES OF THE UNITED STATES,
IN THE FIELD, April 10, 1865.

I. - All officers and men of the Confederate service paroled at Appomattox Court House, Va., who, to reach their homes, are compelled to pass through the lines of the Union armies, will be allowed to do so, and to pass free on all Government transports and military railroads.

II. - Bvt. Gen. R. H. Jackson, U. S. Volunteers, is hereby assigned to duty according to his brevet rank, by authority of the Secretary of War.

By command of Lieutenant-General Grant.
E. S. PARKER,
Lieutenant-Colonel and Acting Assistant Adjutant-General.[405]

This order was given to the Confederate army in the following form:

Special Orders,
No. .....

HEADQUARTERS, ARMY OF NORTHERN VA.
April 10, 1865.

The following order is published for the information of all parties concerned:

Special Orders,
No. .....

HEADQUARTERS, ARMIES OF THE UNITED STATES,
IN THE FIELD, April 10, 1865.

All officers and men of the Confederate service paroled at Appomattox Court House who, to reach their homes are compelled to pass through the lines of the Union Armies, will be allowed to do so, and to pass free on all Government transports and military railroads.

By command of Lieutenant-General Grant:
E. S. PARKER,
Lieutenant-Colonel and Assistant Adjutant-General.
By command of General R. E. LEE.
C. S. VENABLE,
Assistant Adjutant-General.[406]

In addition to the order allowing all home-going Confederates to pass through the Union lines and travel free on Government transports and military railroads, General Grant issued a special order in regard to the movements of General Lee:

This order was as follows:

APPOMATTOX COURT-HOUSE, VA., April 10, 1865.

All officers commanding posts, pickets, or detachments will pass General R. E. Lee through their lines north or south on presentation of this pass. General Lee will be permitted to visit Richmond at any time unless otherwise ordered by competent authority, and every facility for his doing so will be given by officers of the U.S. Army to whom this may be presented.

U. S. GRANT,
Lieutenant-General.[407]

While there is no evidence on this point, it seems likely that Grant told Lee at their conference that such an order would be issued. Here again is to be noted another manifestation of the very generous and courteous treatment which Grant accorded to Lee throughout the whole surrender proceedings at Appomattox Court House.

There is no evidence that Grant and Lee discussed any of the details in connection with the surrender parade on April 12. Even a guess as to whether or not it was discussed does not seem to be justified.

One point which deserves some comment is how much of the conversation between Grant and Lee was heard by the Union officers who were present at the conference. Horace Porter thought that the conference was private and that the two generals were "out of ear-shot."[408] Freeman accepted Porter's statement and said that Grant and Lee were "out of earshot."[409] Badeau stated that the two commanders were "out of hearing."[410] Grant apparently told C. A. Dana, the Assistant Secretary of the War, that he had a "private" conference with Lee.[411]

Grant and Lee apparently did withdraw by themselves during the first part of their conversation, but then there was a considerable period when one or more Union officers took part in the discussion.

Ely Parker said that he served as the secretary for the two generals and that when they "would come to a decision on any point I would write it down." He explained that "there was an old stump and I would stoop over it while I wrote." He described the conference business as "the culmination of the agreements that were entered upon the day before" and "finishing up the business, as it were."[412]

As already noted, Gibbon said that he was beckoned forward to discuss the issuing of paroles and the exemption of certain horses from the surrender. Various other matters might have been discussed and noted by Parker.

The idea that quite a few of the surrender details were discussed by Grant and Lee is given some weight by the fact that Grant spent only an hour at the McLean House following his conference with Lee. During that hour he was visited by many of the officers in both armies and had very little time to discuss surrender details with his commissioners or to ask Parker to prepare official orders. While he was at the McLean House, he probably gave some final instructions to Gibbon, Griffin, and Merritt in regard to drawing up the formal terms of surrender. Grant described his second and last visit to the McLean House as follows:

> When Lee and I separated he went back to his lines and I returned to the house of Mr. McLean. Here the officers of both armies came in great numbers, and seemed to enjoy the meeting as much as though they had been friends separated for a long time while fighting battles under the same flag. For the time being it looked very much as if all thought of the war had escaped their minds. After an hour pleasantly passed in this way I set out on horseback, accompanied by my staff and a small escort, for Burkesville Junction, up to which point the railroad had by this time been repaired.[413]

After their conferences at Appomattox Court House, it seems that Lee and Grant had only one other meeting, which was held in Washington at the White House on May 1, 1869.[414] Different versions of this meeting exist, some claiming that Lee merely made a courtesy call on Grant and others stating that he made several suggestions in regard to policies concerning Virginia and the South. An article in the New York *Times* of January 15, 1912, not cited by Freeman, reported a claim by St. Clair McKelway, an assistant Washington correspondent of the New York *World,* that Lee saw Grant in an effort to prevent military interference in the election of a Virginia governor. Since the interview was private, the exact nature of their conversation will probably remain unknown.

McKelway stated that he talked to Lee in Georgetown at the time of his visit to the White House. "The impression created was a man of great dignity, great simplicity, and precision of statement, without excitement or resentment. There was no bitterness, no recrimination."

Since the names of Lee and Grant are so inseparably linked in American history, it is of considerable significance that Lee probably saw more of Grant while he was at Appomattox Court House than he did at any other place.

LEE'S MEETING WITH G. G. MEADE

On the morning of April 10, following his conference with Grant, Lee had a meeting at his headquarters with Major General G. G. Meade.

Colonel Theodore Lyman, a member of Meade's staff, said that Meade proposed to ride through the Confederate lines to General Grant, who was at Appomattox Court House.[415] There is no evidence that Meade saw Grant or talked with him on this occasion. There is no indication as to why Meade apparently changed his mind about paying a visit to Grant.

Meade was accompanied by his son, Captain George Meade, and Colonel Theodore Lyman. They were escorted to Lee's headquarters by Major General Charles W. Field. After exchanging greetings, Lee took Meade into his tent for a private conference. It was reported that Lee said that Meade asked him about the number of Confederates who were in the lines around Petersburg and was surprised to learn that his forces far outnumbered the men in Lee's command.[416]

If Lee and Meade discussed the surrender or any other matter related to the events at Appomattox, there does not seem to be any record of it.

GENERAL ORDER NUMBER 9

General Order No. 9, General R. E. Lee's farewell order to his troops at Appomattox Court House, has become one of the most famous bits of prose in the English language. A very brief and simple document, it has been said that it "deserves to take its place beside Washington's Farewell Address and Lincoln's Gettysburg Address."[417]

This farewell order was largely the work of Colonel Charles Marshall, the military secretary of General Lee. On the evening of April 9, Lee asked Marshall to prepare an order to the troops which would express Lee's feelings toward his men. About 10 A.M. the following morning, Marshall had not yet been able to complete this task. He gave the following explanation:

> The next day it was raining, and many persons were coming and going, so that I was unable to write without interruption until about 10 o'clock, when General Lee, finding that the order had not been prepared, directed me to get into his ambulance, which stood near his tent, and placed an orderly to prevent any one from approaching me.[418]

Another reason for Marshall's tardiness in preparing this order was probably the fact that he hardly knew what to say. This was indicated in a conversation which he had with F. M. Colston, who had been a fellow-student with him at the Warren Green Academy in Warrenton, Virginia. Colston went to see Marshall about going home, as they were both residents of the City of Baltimore. After a little talk, Marshall said: "Fred Colston, General Lee has told me to write a farewell address. What can I say to these people?"[419] Colston did not say that he gave Marshall any suggestions. He merely decided to leave him alone and let him work it out all by himself.

Marshall said that he sat in General Lee's ambulance until he had made the first draft of the order, which was written in pencil. He then submitted the first draft to General Lee for his approval. Lee struck out an entire paragraph which he thought might help to keep alive a feeling of animosity between the North and the South and also changed one or two other words. There is no record of the exact language which was used in the eliminated paragraph.

Marshall then made a copy of the order as corrected and gave it to one of the clerks in the adjutant-general's office to write in ink.[420]

Norman Bell, a young 19-year-old clerk from Norfolk, Virginia, claimed that he had the honor of making the copy of General Order No. 9.

> After receiving General Lee's approval, Colonel Marshall turned the order over to Norman Bell to have the necessary copies made, one for each corps commander. Bell made an extra copy, which was signed by General Lee along with the others. This copy Bell retained and brought home with him.[421]

General Lee signed a number of copies of General Order No. 9 for his officers and also signed quite a few souvenir copies which men wrote out for themselves and took to General Lee for his signature.[422] General Lee also signed a number of copies during the post-war years. Hence there are a good many so-called "original" copies of General Order No. 9 now in existence.

The real original copy of General Order No. 9, written in pencil by Colonel Marshall and given to Norman Bell to copy, was evidently lost or destroyed and is presumed to be no longer in existence.

Some have thought that a copy of the order in possession of Marshall's descendants might be the revised copy which Marshall handed to Bell. Freeman stated, however, that this copy "cannot be affirmed positively to be the paper given by Marshall to the copyist."[423]

Freeman was willing to state quite positively that the copy of the order in possession of Marshall's descendants was "in Marshall's autograph".[424]

It seems that this statement cannot be accepted. A careful analysis of this copy by handwriting experts has shown that it is definitely not in Marshall's handwriting.[425] It must be regarded as simply another souvenir copy. This reinforces the judgment already stated that there is no original copy (Marshall's copy in pencil).

Quite a few different versions of General Order No. 9 are now in existence, so that there is some doubt about which version should be regarded as the "official" version.

Freeman did not discuss the merits of the different versions. He reproduced the text of the order from General Lee's letter book, into which it was copied, after Appomattox, by Custis Lee.[426] There are several objections to this copy. It has four paragraphs instead of five and uses the word "Orders" instead of "Order". It uses the capitalized word "Country" instead of "countrymen".

Morris Schaff printed a version of General Order No. 9 in *The Sunset of the Confederacy.* This version has only three paragraphs; it has "would have attended" instead of "must have attended"; the words "merciful" and "his", referring to the Deity, are not capitalized.[427]

In 1866, Henderson and Company published General Order No. 9 in connection with a Map of Appomattox Court House and Vicinity. This was reprinted by the National Park Service as "a document so nearly contemporary with the surrender." This version has five paragraphs, but it has "would have attended" instead of "must have attended" and does not capitalize "merciful" when referring to the Deity. The objectionable features of this version are fewer in number than is generally true.

Two versions of Order No. 9 were printed in the *Official Records.* Neither one is regarded as authentic. The first has only three paragraphs; it has "Orders" instead of "Order"; it does not capitalize "His" when referring to the Deity.[428] The second is all in one paragraph; it has "Orders" instead of "Order"; it uses "may have attended" instead of "must have attended"; it does not capitalize "His" when referring to the Diety.[429]

There are objections to the order published by Marshall in *Battles and Leaders.* This copy has only three paragraphs; it uses "would have attended" instead of "must have attended"; it does not capitalize "His" when referring to the Deity.[430]

The copy in the possession of the relatives of Norman Bell is very close to the authentic text. The only objection seems to be that words "His" and "Merciful" are not capitalized when referring to the Deity.[431]

The copy printed in some Southern newspapers soon after the surrender has only four paragraphs; "would have attended" is used instead of "must have attended"; and the words "His" and "Merciful" are not capitalized.[432]

After an extended study of Order No. 9, J. E. Fields decided that the most authentic text and paragraphing were in the copy of the order addressed to Walter Husted Stevens the Chief Engineer of the Army of Northern Virginia. This copy of the order is written on a folic sheet of blue paper of English manufacture.[433]

The text and paragraphing approved by Fields were also selected by Dowdey and Manarin for their recent edition of *The Wartime Papers of R. E. Lee.* It is believed that this represents the most authentic text and paragraphing and is as follows:

GENERAL ORDER, NO. 9
Headquarters, Army of Northern Virginia
April 10, 1865

After four years of arduous service, marked by unsurpassed courage and fortitude, the Army of Northern Virginia has been compelled to yield to overwhelming numbers and resources.

I need not tell the brave survivors of so many hard fought battles, who have remained steadfast to the last, that I have consented to this result from no distrust of them.

But feeling that valor and devotion could accomplish nothing that would compensate for the loss that must have attended the continuance of the contest, I determined to avoid the useless sacrifice of those whose past services have endeared them to their countrymen.

By the terms of the agreement officers and men can return to their homes and remain until exchanged. You will take with you the satisfaction that proceeds from the consciousness of duty faithfully performed, and I earnestly pray that a Merciful God will extend to you His blessing and protection.

With an increasing admiration of your constancy and devotion to your country, and a grateful remembrance of your kind and generous considerations for myself, I bid you all an affectionate farewell.

R. E. LEE
Genl.[434]

Some have thought that printed copies of General Order No. 9 might have been struck off in the vicinity of Appomattox Court House a few days after the surrender. A printed copy, said to be printed on contemporary paper with contemporary type, is in existence, but the evidence for the production of printed copies at Appomattox is considered much too slight to prove this point.[435] Wherever it might have been printed, the paragraphing and text of this copy cannot be regarded as authentic.

General Order No. 9 was read to the Confederate troops when they were drawn in their final formations. While all of the accounts do not mention this, it is presumed that this practice was generally followed. William A. Owen, adjutant of the Washington Artillery of New Orleans, said that he assembled the men in his battalion and read Lee's farewell order to them. He stated: "The men listened with marked attention and with moistened eyes as the grand farewell from their old chief was read."[436]

Lee's farewell order undoubtedly struck a responsive chord in the hearts of his troops and was sincerely treasured and acclaimed by all of his men. Colonel Elijah V. White, the leader of the famous Laurel Cavalry troop, is said to have carried a copy of the order in his wallet until the day of his death.[437]

Eugene Henry Levy, a Confederate soldier from Louisiana, copied General Order No. 9 in his diary and then wrote the following words:

> Hope yet remains, and when the Lilly of France is borne against the grasping Eagle the name of our venerated chief will act as a talisman to call the sons of the South once more to strive for national independence. God grant that the day is not far distant.[438]

Writing near the turn of the century, George A. Forsyth said that "to this day, no old soldier of the Army of Northern Virginia can read (General Order No. 9) without moistening eyes and swelling throat."[439]

Ellsworth Eliot, Jr., pointed out that the wording of General Order No. 9 would have needed very little revision even if the situation had been reversed, and General Lee had been the victor instead of the one who had suffered defeat. Eliot said: "Under such different circumstances the beautiful language of his farewell address to his soldiers would have required only slight modification, the last two paragraphs none at all."[440]

PAROLING THE ARMY OF NORTHERN VIRGINIA

It had been agreed at the conference between Grant and Lee on the morning of April 10 that each Confederate would be provided with a parole pass, and John Gibbon had promised to try to print the blank certificates on a small Union army press which he had with him. He gave the following description of how the blank parolees were printed:

> My corps press was at once set to work to print off the requisite number of blank paroles, but it soon became apparent that our few printers would speedily break down at the task, some thirty thousand being required. The adjutant-general reported that the press would have to be run all night and probably all the next day. I therefore directed him to send out and

make a detail from the corps of the requisite number of printers to supply relays for the press until the job was finished. This was done, and we obtained all the printers we wanted, and the next day the paroles were ready for distribution. If we had needed fifty watchmakers or blacksmiths I presume we could have had them just as readily.[441]

The little Union army printing press broke down before all the paroles could be printed, and a manuscript source used by Freeman indicated that the paroles of some individuals had to be printed in Lynchburg.[442] Unfortunately, at least one writer was misled by the wording of Freeman's statement and said that all the paroles were "hastily ground out on presses at nearby Lynchburg."[443]

The parole passes had the following wording:

Appomattox Court House, Va.,
April 10th, 1865

The bearer, ______________________________,

of Co. ____________________, Regt. ______________,

of ______________________, a Paroled Prisoner of the Army of Northern Virginia, has permission to go to his home, and there remain undisturbed.

Some passes had "Paroled Prisoner's Pass" printed vertically across the left end. There was a difference in the decorative designs on the left end of the passes, some having one design and some another.

These parole passes were signed either by a prisoner's own commander or his commander's staff officer.[444] Several passes which were issued to men at Appomattox Court House are in the files at ACHNHP.

Confederate commanding officers were allowed to sign paroles of honor on behalf of the men in their commands, certifying that the men on the parole lists would not take up arms against the United States until properly exchanged.

These paroles of honor were worded as follows:

I, the undersigned, commanding officer of ______________ ______________, do, for the within named prisoners of war, belonging to the Army of Northern Virginia, who have been this day surrendered by General Robert E. Lee, C. S. A., commanding said army, to Lieutenant-General U. S. Grant, commanding Armies of the United States, hereby give my solemn parole of honor that the within named shall not hereafter serve in the armies of the Confederate States, or in any military capacity whatever against the United States of America, or render aid to

> the enemies of the latter until properly exchanged, in such manner as shall be mutually approved by the respective authorities.
>
> Done at Appomattox Court House, Va., this 9th day of April, 1865.[445]

This form was evidently printed on the back of the duplicate rolls of the surrendered troops. John Gibbon said:

> Rolls in duplicate had been prepared of the different commands, and on the back of these was placed a blank form of parole, to be duly filled out and signed by the commanding officer. Such officers as did not belong to any party organization signed a different form of parole.[446]

General Lee and his staff officers signed a parole of honor with the following wording:

> We, the undersigned Prisoners of War, belonging to the army of Northern Virginia, having been this day surrendered by General Robert E. Lee, C. S. A., Commanding said Army, to Lieut. Genl. U. S. Grant, Commanding Armies of United States, do hereby give our solemn parole of honor that we will not hereafter serve in the armies of the Confederate States, or in any military capacity whatever, against the United States of America, or render aid to the enemies of the latter, until properly exchanged, in such manner as shall be mutually approved by the respective authorities.
>
> Done at Appomattox Court)
> House, Va., this 9th day of)
> April, 1865)
>
> This parole carried the indorsement of George H. Sharpe.[447]

In accordance with the surrender terms proposed by Grant on April 9, rolls of all the officers and men were made out in duplicate, one copy for a Union officer and one for the Confederates.[448]

Grant appointed Bvt. Brig. Gen. George H. Sharpe, assistant provost-marshall-general, to receive and take charge of the parole lists on behalf of the Union Army.[449]

The work of making up the parole lists of Confederate troops was started on April 10,[450] and on that day, members of artillery units began to turn over their guns, ammunition, and other equipment to Turner's Independent Division of the XXIV Union Army Corps, which was stationed near the Court House.[451]

Freeman said that the formal surrender of the artillery was put first, because the horses of the batteries were dying for lack of feed.[452]

Although the artillerymen did not go through the same sort of ceremony which was later required of the infantry, they were drawn up in a final formation on April 11. Lieutenant Colonel W. T. Poague gave the following description of the disbanding of his battalion:

> Tuesday morning farewells and goodbyes were said, the battalion was formed in line, general orders read and the last command given: "The Battalion is disbanded!" The companies soon were out of sight. How long they kept together as companies I know not; probably they soon broke up into small squads.
>
> I had thought of saying a few things to the battalion when last drawn up in the way of expressing my appreciation of their fine soldierly qualities ever since I had the honor to command them, especially in the recent trying days. But I found myself dumb — so utterly and unexpectedly overcome that I broke down at the very start - and was able only to utter in broken tones: "Men, Farewell!" I speak truly when I say there has never been a day since, when I could dwell on that last scene without experiencing emotions of deepest grief and sorrow.[453]

Carlton McCarthy, a private in Cutshaw's artillery battalion, left the following description of the departure of his unit:

> Captain Fry, who commanded after Colonel Cutshaw was wounded, assembled the battalion, thanked the men for their faithfulness, bid them farewell, and read the following (General Order No. 9). This grand farewell from the man who had in the past personified the glory of his army, and now bore its grief in his own great heart, was the signal for tearful partings. Comrades wept as they gazed upon each other, and with choking voices said, farewell! And so - they parted. Little groups of two or three or four, without food, without money, but with "the satisfaction that proceeds from the consciousness of duty faithfully performed," were soon plodding their way homeward.[454]

Comparatively speaking, the number of artillerymen paroled at Appomattox Court House was not large, the total being only 2,576.[455]

The number of cavalrymen was even smaller, a total of 1,559.[456] This figure is from the parole lists and does not mean that this many men were actually present when the formal surrender took place. A rather small group of men in W. H. F. Lee's command might have been the only ones who were present when the time came to surrender the cavalry sabers and the accouterments to Ronald MacKenzie's troops. On April 10 the following order was sent to MacKenzie:

> The major-general commanding directs that you will send, without delay, one brigade of your command to the road north of the Appomattox Court-House, for the purpose of receiving the sabers, accouterments, &c., of the cavalry of the Confederate army surrendered to the United States on the 9th instant. They will be placed in position by Major Embler, aide-de-camp, who will be on the road. The brigade will remain in position all night.[457]

No detailed descriptions of the surrender of the cavalry have been discovered during the research carried on for this study. The final cavalry formation was probably similar to the artillery formations described by Poague and McCarthy.

The formal surrender of the artillerymen and cavalrymen took place on the morning of April 11. A confederate private who had been captured on the night of April 8 and taken to a prison "pen" near Appomattox Station said that it was another "foggy gloomy day; the very heavens seem to sympathize with my humour and my country's agony." He also related: "In the afternoon, some of the cavalry passed bye (sic) the pen, on their way home to remain neutral until exchanged."[458]

At noon on April 11 Turner's Division and MacKenzie's cavalry were relieved by Bartlett's First Division of the V Union Army Corps, the unit which had been selected to receive the formal surrender of the infantry.[459]

Around midnight on April 10 Brigadier General J. L. Chamberlain was called to division headquarters and informed that "General Grant had appointed me to take charge of this (surrender) parade and to receive the formal surrender of the guns and flags."[460]

Freeman said that Maj. General Charles Griffin awarded this honor to Chamberlain.[461] Chamberlain wrote several accounts of his experiences at Appomattox, and at another place said that Griffin "informed" him that he was to command the surrender parade,[462] but did not say that Grant appointed him. Freeman apparently was using an account which did not mention Grant's appointment.

Chamberlain said that he thought his appointment was more of an honor for the V Corps than for him and that he believed Griffin had something to do with Grant's kind remembrance.[463]

Chamberlain conferred with both Griffin and Gibbon about the surrender parade.[464] Wesley Merritt, the other Union commissioner, was not present at this conference. Griffin explained Grant's wishes and "added in a significant tone that Grant wished the ceremony to be as simple as possible, and that nothing should be done to humiliate the manhood of the Southern soldiers."[465]

Chamberlain said that he regretted that the II and VI Army Corps did not have a share in the surrender parade. "We could not but feel something more than a wish that they should be brought up to be participants in a consummation to which they perhaps more than any had contributed."[466]

Chamberlain's description of the surrender parade is on a moving and eloquent account of the notable events on April 12, and one is tempted to quote his entire narrative. Although no summary can do justice to his words, a summary is given here instead of extended quotations.

Chamberlain had been ordered to have his lines formed for the ceremony at sunrise. It was a chilly, gray morning. The Confederates were stationed on the hill beyond the valley and the Union soldiers were on the hill east of the Court House, so that each body of soldiers could see the other.

The Union line extended along both sides of the Richmond-Lynchburg Stage Road from the Northern Branch of the Appomattox River all the way to the McLean House. A member of the 118th Pennsylvania (Corn Exchange) Regiment said that the 118th was near the fence which enclosed the ground surrounding the McLean House.[467]

Freeman said that the line extended "to the Court House."[468] John J. Pullen thought that it went "almost to the Court House on the left".[469]

Some markers indicating the right and left flanks of the Union line were erected by the U. S. War Department about 1890. The marker indicating the left flank is some distance east of the Court House.

According to Chamberlain's account, the 155th Pennsylvania was apparently on the left of the 118th Pennsylvania. This would have made the left of the line extend even beyond the McLean House. Chamberlain said that the Third Brigade was composed of the following troops:

> In the Third Brigade line there were regiments representing the states of Maine, Massachusetts, Michigan, and Pennsylvania, regiments which had been through the entire war. The Bay State veterans had the right of the line down the village street. This was 32d Massachusetts Regiment, with some members of the 9th, 18th, and 22d Regiments. Next in order came the First Maine Sharpshooters, the 20th Regiment, and some of the 2d. There were also the First Michigan Sharpshooters, the 1st and 16th Regiments, and some men of the 4th, Pennsylvania was represented by the 83d, the 91st, the 118th, and the 155th.[470]

There were two other brigades in Bartlett's First Division of the V Union Army Corps. The First Brigade was composed of the 198th Pennsylvania and the 185th New York. The Second Brigade was made up of the 187th, the 188th, and the 189th New York.[471]

The Third Brigade was on the side of the road next to the Court House; the Second Brigade was across the street; the First Brigade was a little to the rear of the Third.[472]

Chamberlain thought that Bartlett, the senior general, was somewhat bothered because Chamberlain was now in command of the division and Bartlett had no troops to command. It is said that Bartlett rode around the surrender area most of the day with his division staff and flag, talking with Confederate officers.[473]

Across the river, the Union troops could see the Confederates breaking up their camp, taking down shelter tents, and getting into formation. Then they marched across the stream. Some of the flag staffs were bare, some flags were tightly bound to the staffs, but many were flying. Chamberlain said:

> On they came, with the old swinging route step, and swaying battle-flags. In the van, the proud Confederate ensign, - the great field of white and for canton the star-strewn cross of blue on a field of red, this latter escutcheon also the regimental battle-flags - following on crowded so thick, by thinning out of men, that the whole column seemed crowned with red. At the right of our line our little group mounted beneath our flags, the red maltese cross on a field of white, erewhile so bravely borne through many a field more crimson than itself, its mystic meaning now ruling all.
>
> This was the last scene of such momentous history that I was impelled to render some token of recognition; some honor also to manhood so high.[474]

Chamberlain had already given instructions to his regimental commanders, and when the head of the Confederate column was opposite the right of the Third Brigade, a bugle sounded, and the Union troops gave the soldier's salutation, the marching salute. John B. Gordon, riding at the head of the Confederate column in a disconsolate manner with his head bowed, suddenly caught the meaning and the spirit of the occasion immediately changed. Gordon wheeled his horse toward the Third Brigade, and while uplifted on his steed dropped his sword point to the toe of his boot and returned Chamberlain's compliment. He then ordered his troops to return the Union salute.[475]

The Union troops were impressed with Gordon's appearance. One man said that "Gen'l Gordon is the best-looking soldier I ever saw in my life."[476]

The Confederates lined up about twelve feet across the road from the Third Brigade, dressed their line, fixed bayonets, stepped forward, stacked arms, and laid down their cartridge boxes. More than anything else they seemed to hate to give up their flags, and many of the men kissed their flags with tears in their eyes.[477]

Freeman thought that Chamberlain was mistaken in saying that the Confederates laid their colors on the ground, and believed that Walter Montgomery of North Carolina "doubtless was correct in stating that the flags were placed on the stacks."[478] Here again, however, Freeman seemed to have used only one of Chamberlain's accounts. Elsewhere Chamberlain said:

> Then, slowly and with a reluctance that was appealingly pathetic, the torn and tattered battleflags were either leaned against the stacks or laid upon the ground.[479]

It seems likely that the Confederates would have had some variation in their manner of surrendering their colors.

The surrendered arms were removed by Union wagons during the intervals of the surrender parade and the cartridge-boxes were emptied in the street when the ammunition was found unserviceable. In the dusk of the evening the long lines of scattered cartridges were set on fire.[480]

According to Chamberlain, the surrender parade occupied nearly the entire day. The Second Confederate Corps was the first to lay down its arms, followed by the Third and First.[481]

The Union troops were not unaffected by the proceedings.

> And it can well be imagined, too, that there was no lack of emotion on our side, but the Union men were held steadily in their lines, without the least show of demonstration by word or by motion. There was, though, a twitching of the muscles of their faces, and, be it said, their battle-bronzed cheeks were not altogether dry. Our men felt the import of the occasion, and realized fully how they would have been affected if defeat and surrender had been their lot after such a fearful struggle.[482]

Chamberlain emphasized the silence which prevailed during the surrender parade.

> On our part not a sound of trumpet more, nor roll of drum; not a cheer, nor word nor whisper of vain-glorying, nor motion of man standing again at the order; but an awed stillness rather and breath-holding, as if it were the passing of the dead![483]

Although Chamberlain's account seems to be generally reliable, and is certainly the most eloquent description of the surrender parade on record, his statement about an "awed stillness" and "breath-holding" cannot be taken literally. There was evidently no hilarious cheering, but there was some conversation and some good-natured banter, as was reported by a member of the 118 Pennsylvania (Corn Exchange) Regiment.

> No conversation was allowed between the two armies while the surrender was being made, but occasionally a pleasant word would be exchanged. One of a regiment which stacked its arms in front of us asked: "What regiment are youuns?" "The 118th Pennsylvania," was the reply. "Didn't we give it to you at Shepherdstown?" came back. "It took a whole rebel division to do it," we replied.[484]

Members of this same Pennsylvania regiment reported that the soldiers in both armies had a little fun during the surrender parade at the expense of Brigadier General Henry A. Wise. Wise drew up his men in front of the 118th Pennsylvania and abused his command for being tardy about dressing their line. Some of his men angrily replied: "Look at him! He is brave enough now, but he never was so near the Yankees before in his life." When the Pennsylvanians learned who Wise was, they joined in the tauntings and shouted: "Who hung John Brown?" "Where did you steal your coat?" "Hang him to a sour apple tree!" "Shoot him!"[485]

It should be said that the 118th Pennsylvania was on the extreme left of the Union line, near the McLean House, and Chamberlain probably did not hear this exchange from his position on the extreme right of the line.[486]

Numbers of the Confederate infantrymen who were at Appomattox evidently did not stay to take part in the surrender parade. They simply threw down their muskets and walked away. The 118th Pennsylvania reported:

> Much work was left for us to do after the rebs had left, in gathering up the stores and munitions of war. In the woods where the rebel army had encamped, muskets were scattered upon the ground in every direction. We found where whole battalions had stacked their arms and left for home, taking no part in the surrender, not even signing their parole. . . . It was a thankless and wearisome job for us to gather up those munitions of war. Major Jos. Ashbrook, who was division ordnance officer, destroyed immense quantities of them.[487]

The number of Confederate infantry paroled at Appomattox totalled 22,349, with 1,747 additional men being among the headquarters and miscellaneous troops. The grand total of all services was 28,231.[488]

Neither Lee nor Grant witnessed the surrender parade on April 12. Grant left Appomattox Court House on the afternoon of April 10, but Lee did not leave until April 12. His official report to President Jefferson Davis, as printed in the Official Records, carries the heading: "Near Appomattox Court-House, Va., April 12, 1865."[489] The date on this report seems to be decisive proof that General Lee did not leave the Appomattox area until

April 12. There are various accounts which list some other day as the time of Lee's departure, but it is believed that they may be safely disregarded.

John Gibbon wrote Grant that the surrender of Lee's army was completed on April 13. His dispatch, dated at Appomattox Court House on April 13, 1865, said:

> The surrender of General Lee's army was finally completed to-day. We have paroled from 25,000 to 30,000 men. One hundred and forty-seven pieces artillery have been received, about 10,000 small arms, and 71 flags. I received on the 11th a deputation from Lynchburg, proposing the surrender of that place and asking for our protection. I started Turner's division and MacKenzie's cavalry for that point yesterday morning. I have conversed with many of the surrendered officers and am satisfied that by announcing at once terms and a liberal, merciful policy on the part of the Government we can once more have a happy, united country. I believe all reasoning men on both sides recognize the fact that slavery is dead.[490]

E. P. Alexander spoke in a complimentary fashion about the way in which the Union officers handled the surrender details.

> Looked at merely as a business proceeding, the simple method of paroling the Confederate army and taking charge of its surrendered property was admirably short and effective.[491]

There were some Confederates, however, who had considerable difficulty in securing their parole passes, because the blank forms ran out. J. H. Claiborne reported that he saw men still in camp awaiting their papers on Friday, April 14.[492] It is believed that virtually all the Confederates finally left Appomattox Court House on that day.

For some reason, hundreds of Confederate prisoners, who were at Appomattox Station on April 9, were not allowed to participate in the surrender at Appomattox Court House. Instead, they were taken to Farmville and paroled there. Eugene Henry Levy, who was captured on the night of April 8 at Appomattox Court House, was in this group. He said that he was paroled at Farmville on April 14 in the following manner:

> Having been formed in line in front of the Provost Marshall's office, the ceremony of paroling commenced. Col. Wilson (Judge Advocate 2nd Corps) facilitated the business for the Louisianians and in an hour the necessary papers had been procured and the oath not to bear arms administered. I got an order for one day's rations of sugar and coffee but the commissary was so indifferent to my business that I left in disgust.[493]

Fitz Lee, accompanied by most of Munford's and Rosser's cavalrymen, rode away from Appomattox Court House on April 9. Munford and Rosser attempted to keep up the struggle for a while,[494] but Fitz Lee soon came back to Appomattox Court House to ask for a parole. John Gibbon described his somewhat dramatic return as follows:

> The next day (April 12), while seated in the McLean House, I received a message saying that General Lee was at the door and would like to see me. I told the messenger to ask him in, but he came back to say that the general declined to dismount. Going to the door, I found General *Fitz* Lee seated on his horse, and looking, I thought, somewhat uneasy. He had been a cadet under me at West Point, and I had not seen him for years. As I looked at him a vision of the past came up before me, and I could only think of a little rollicking fellow dressed in *cadet* gray whose jolly songs and gay spirits were the life of his class. My salutation of "Hello, Fitz! Get off and come in," seemed to put him at ease at once, and brought him to his feet. He came into the house and told his story. Early on the 9th, seeing that surrender was inevitable, he had, with his cavalry force, made his escape and proceeded toward Lynchburg; but becoming convinced that the war was virtually ended, he rode to Farmville and reported to General Meade. He was advised to return to Appomattox and be paroled. He became my guest for the night, and, lying on the floor, slept as soundly as a child, after, as he said, having had no sleep for a week. Nothing could dampen his high spirits, and with us he seemed to rejoice that the war was over. With a grim humor, he took from his pocket a five-dollar Confederate note, and writing across its face, "For Mrs. Gibbon, with the compliments of Fitz Lee," he said: "Send that to your wife, and tell her it's the last cent I have in the world."[495]

Confederates who left Appomattox Court House without being paroled continued to come in and ask for their paroles for a number of weeks. George Taylor Lee, a nephew of General R. E. Lee, and a member of Munford's cavalry, stayed in the mountains near Roanoke, Virginia, until the first part of May and then decided to go to Richmond and give himself up and be paroled. When he reached the proper office, he "saw that many others were wanting to get their papers and that I would have to wait a long time, maybe many hours, before I could get mine. However, there was nothing else to do, so I took my place at the end of a long line of men, who seemed to be moving up very slowly indeed."[496]

Paroles were issued at Richmond, Farmville, Lynchburg and other places on the same basis as those which were given at Appomattox Court House. Major General E. O. C. Ord issued an order on April 14 which directed that this should be done. He said: "I have issued an order that any rebels coming and giving themselves up will be paroled on the same terms as Lee's army."[497]

CONFEDERATE REACTION TO THE CLOSE OF HOSTILITIES AND THE SURRENDER

Although Lee's general officers had anticipated the end of organized resistance on the part of the Army of Northern Virginia, many of the lower officers and men in the ranks did not seem to realize that the end was rapidly approaching. One Confederate captain reported that "even the stragglers expected Lee to carry them off safely" and that "many thought that the genius of Lee would yet triumph."[498]

Being unprepared for such news, many were shocked and stunned when they saw the flags of truce and became aware that they would soon be prisoners of war. Colonel W. W. Blackford said that it struck him "like an electric shock." He recalled that the "effect was like that of a stunning blow, and for a moment I felt dazzed . . .".[499]

James R. Hagood emphasized the feeling of shock which the Confederates experienced.

> The emotion which the news produced can only be imagined — I cannot describe it. We looked in each other's faces, where blank and fathomless despair was written, nor said one word -our hearts were too full for language. We vainly strove to comprehend the reality of our situation but our intellects were stunned by the heaviness of the blow and we could only murmur stupidly and meaninglessly the word "surrendered"! It sounded like a knell of damnation.[500]

W. T. Poague gave a very graphic description of the sorrow which fell upon the Army of Northern Virginia on April 9.

> Such scenes as followed were never before witnessed in the old Army of Northern Virginia. Men expressed in various ways the agonizing emotions that shook their souls and broke their hearts. Some cried like children. Others sat on the ground with faces buried in hands, quietly sobbing. Others embraced friends, their bodies trembling and shaking. Others, struck dumb and with blanched faces, seemed to strain their eyes to catch the form of some awful horror that suddenly loomed before them. But it is useless for me to try to picture the gloom and sorrow of that supreme moment.[501]

Carlton McCarthy said: "Many of the men were sobbing and crying, like children recovering from convulsions of grief after a severe whipping. They were sorely grieved, mortified, and humiliated. Of course they had not the slightest conception of the numbers of the enemy who surrounded them."[502]

There were many who were not able to recall anything except the sadness of Appomattox and the grief which they experienced. T. J. Macon, a member of the First Company of Richmond Howitzers, said: "I don't think there was a cannoneer in line who did not grieve at the fact of our defeat. Men who had gone into battle and faced danger with unflinching nerve were moved to tears at our sad disaster. ...It was the saddest day of my life."[503]

Perhaps the comments of others were mellowed by the passing of the years. Edward A. Moore stated: "The favorable and entirely unexpected terms of surrender wonderfully restored our souls; and at once plans, first for returning to our homes, and then for starting life anew, afforded ample interest and entertainment."[504]

All the varieties of human emotion must have been experienced in one way or another by the Confederates at Appomattox. Carlton McCarthy reported that a lieutenant in his battalion was "surprised, disgusted, indignant, and incredulous. . .".[505]

It probably took some little time for the significance of the surrender to impress itself upon the minds of the Confederate soldiers at Appomattox.

E. P. Alexander said:

> I think the full moral effect of the surrender was hardly felt until the next morning, being obscured by the excitement attendant upon it. The next day seemed to usher in a new life in a new world. We had lived through the war. There was nobody trying to shoot us, and nobody for us to shoot at. Our guns were gone, our country was gone, our very entity seemed to be destroyed. We were no longer soldiers, and had no orders to obey, nothing to do, and nowhere to go.[506]

UNION CELEBRATIONS OF THE END OF HOSTILITIES AND OF THE SURRENDER

Union troops went wild with joy when they knew that hostilities had come to an end. Many descriptions of their exuberant celebrations were recorded by those who were present at Appomattox Court House.

Private Charles E. Dunn of the 20th Maine Regiment recalled that in his regiment "muskets, knapsacks, haversacks, canteens, dippers, everything that a man could get his hands on went into the air" and that men were laughing, shouting, shaking hands, hugging each other and even crying.[507]

J. L. Chamberlain's description of the reaction of his troops was:

> To the top of fences, and haystacks, and chimneys they clamber, to toss their old caps higher in the air, and leave the earth as far below them as they can. Dear old General Gregory gallops up to inquire the meaning of this strange departure from accustomed discipline. "Only that Lee wants time to surrender," I answer with stage solemnity. "Glory to God!" roars the grave and brave old General, dashing upon me with impetuosity that nearly unhorsed us both, to grasp and wring my hand, which had not yet had time to lower the sword. "Yes, and on earth peace; good will towards men." I answered, bringing the thanksgiving from heavenward, manward.[508]

Surgeon Alphonso D. Rockwell, who was with Sheridan's Cavalry, said that as the white flag was borne out toward the Union troops their "cheers echoed and re-echoed through the morning air at the thought of peace!"[509]

A newspaper dispatch mentioned that the Union army bands in the Fifth Corps began to play "the national airs with a strength of nerve truly astonishing."[510]

Some men in the Union army celebrated the cessation of hostilities with tears rather than with shouts of joy. It is said that Brigadier General Alfred Gibbs broke down and sobbed whenever he realized that the bloodshed was almost over.[511]

Much of the Union shouting at the close of hostilities was probably not within hearing distance of the Confederate troops, because virtually none of the Confederate accounts of the surrender mention any cheering by the Union troops.

When the surrender was officially announced at 4 P.M., there was a new outburst of cheering among the members of the Union army, especially in the II and VI Corps.

Brevet Major General Nelson A. Miles declared:

> The air was filled with hats, canteens, haversacks and everything that could be displayed as an expression of great rejoicing. The grim warriors embraced each other and rolled over on the turf with tears of joy coursing down their bronzed faces.[512]

Some of the colored troops near the Court House became so excited that they decided to fire "an exultant volley, much to the surprise of their less demonstrative and better disciplined white comrades."[513]

Sometime later, the sound of the regular firing of cannon was heard in the distance. Someone said: "The Army of the Potomac has heard of Lee's surrender and is firing a salute in honor of our victory."[514]

The firing of salutes was displeasing to Grant, who sent word to have it stopped. He said: "The Confederates were now our prisoners, and we did not want to exult over their downfall."[515]

Union bands began to play the national airs, such as "Hail Columbia" and "The Star Spangled Banner".[516]

Many Union men sat down to write letters home. A letter from an unknown Union soldier to his mother was as follows:

Appomattox Court House
April 9th, 1865

My Dear Mother:

I am almost too much excited to write. You will know the reason why long before you receive this. Lee has surrendered with his whole army, and from this day the war is virtually over. Thank God we have been permitted to see this glorious day. Johnston's army will certainly surrender and, then, dear Mother, we will all return home again to enjoy the blessings of that *honorable* peace for which we have striven so long. The men of Lee's army have torn down their works, stacked their arms and are now encamped quietly alongside of us as though they formed part of our army. As soon as the arrangements for the surrender were made officers and messengers bore the news to the troops and, oh, what a scene! All the pent up emotions of our hearts burst forth in a mighty shout, like the shout of battle, while the bands struck up our national airs and the artillery broke forth in salutes. How the hats of the boys flew skyward in the air and the hills fairly shook with the cheers of the massed thousands, when General Meade, with uncovered head and beaming face, rode down the lines with the glorious news. We have orders to remain here, close in camp, until it is settled what will be done. Good night, my dear Mother, and look for our return "when Johnny comes marching home".[517]

REACTION TO THE TERMS OF SURRENDER

On the Confederate side, the reaction to the terms of surrender offered by Grant was more than favorable. Both officers and men expressed their gratitude for the consideration which they received, as well as some surprise.

E. P. Alexander wrote as follows:

My story would be very incomplete did I not refer to the manner in which our exceedingly liberal treatment by Grant was regarded. It was, in the first place, a great surprise, for

> Grant had never before given any terms to an opponent. Now he seemed anxious to give us everything we could ask for. We knew our inferiority in force and our desperate condition too well to ascribe it to any hesitation to give us battle again. The generosity of his terms could only be ascribed to a policy of conciliation deliberately entered upon. Of course we were sore and mortified, so much so that we had not much to say to any one; but it put everybody in some sort of hope that, after all, defeat might not mean utter destruction.[518]

Edward A. Moore, a member of the Rockbridge Artillery, probably voiced the feelings of many rank and file Confederates when he said:

> By noon, or soon thereafter, the terms of the surrender were made known - terms so generous, considerate, and unlooked-for as scarcely believed to be possible. None of that exposure to the gaze and exultation of a victorious foe, such as we had seen pictured in our schoolbooks, or as practiced by conquering nations in all times. We had felt it as not improbable that, after an ordeal of mortifying exposure for the gratification of the military, we would be paraded through Northern cities for the benefit of jeering crowds. So, when we learned that we should be paroled, and go to our homes unmolested, the relief was unbounded.[519]

All the Confederates were especially pleased because Grant consented to allow artillerymen and cavalrymen to retain their privately-owned horses. Chamberlain said:

> Praises of General Grant were on every tongue for his magnanimity in allowing the horses of the artillery and cavalry that were the property of the men and not of the Confederacy, to be retained by the men for service in restoring and working the little plantations, and also in requesting the managers of transportation companies in all that region to facilitate in every way the return of these men to their homes.[520]

While Grant's generosity at Appomattox Court House was highly extolled by the Confederates, he was even more generous than is generally recognized. His own experience as a poor farmer probably led him to be sympathetic for the poverty-stricken farmers in and around Appomattox Court House. He issued an order to Gibbon in which Gibbon was instructed to move most of his supplies from Appomattox Court House by way of the railroad and to leave the captured wagons at the Court House for the country people to pick up.[521]

He also told Gibbon to appropriate what his command needed out of the public stores at Lynchburg and then distribute the balance "among the poor of the city".[522]

The Union troops left much more than wagons behind when they finally left the vicinity of Appomattox Court House. George W. Munford said that

> They left great numbers of wagons and gear, spades, picks, shovels, iron of every description suitable for farm purposes, trace chains and a great many other useful things, besides many broken down horses and mules.[523]

While they were still at Appomattox Court House, many Confederates must have expressed their appreciation to Grant for his generosity. C. A. Dana, the assistant Secretary of War, was apparently repeating what Grant had told him when he (Dana) sent a message to Edwin M. Stanton on April 12 saying: "All were greatly impressed by the generosity of the terms finally given them, for at the time of the surrender they were surrounded and escape was impossible."[524]

Senator E. B. Washburne, who was with the Union army at Appomattox, sent a telegram to President Lincoln on April 15 which said: "I am just from Appomattox Court-House, where I saw the entire rebel army lay down their arms. I talked with a large number of their officers, and found a much better spirit than I had anticipated."[525]

The attitude of the men in the Union army was generally friendly towards the Confederates. E. P. Alexander said that "Grant's policy of conciliation was followed by every one in his army, even to the teamsters along the roads."[526] It is therefore presumed that most of the Union men were pleased that Grant offered generous terms to the Confederates.

Charles C. Coffin, however, indicated that there were some men in the Union army who objected because Grant granted generous terms to certain Confederate officers.

> The soldiers idolized Grant as a commander. They had no objection to his terms with the privates of Lee's army, but there was dissent from including Pickett and Ewell, and other Rebel officers who had been notoriously inhuman in Union soldiers.[527]

Coffin was especially critical of the lenient treatment accorded to Pickett, because Pickett had ordered the execution of a number of North Carolinians who were captured by the Confederates after they enlisted in the Union army. Pickett said that he executed these men because he regarded them as traitors. Coffin argued that Pickett should have been treated as a traitor because he enlisted in the Confederate army without resigning his commission in the Army of the United States.[528]

It is not believed that Union criticism of the generosity of Grant's surrender terms was very widespread, because references like the ones found in Coffin's book seem to be rather rare.

THE SURRENDER IN THE REPORTS OF CONFEDERATE OFFICERS

After the surrender at Appomattox Court House, General Lee sent a communication to his general officers asking for a short report of the operations of their commands from "the time of the recent attacks of the enemy near Petersburg to the present".

The following is a copy of the letter received by G. E. Pickett:

HEADQUARTERS ARMY OF NORTHERN VIRGINIA,
April 10, 1865.

GENERAL: General Lee wishes you to make at once a short report of the operations of your command from the time of the recent attacks of the enemy near Petersburg to the present. He desires you also to call upon the commanders of the divisions which were assigned to you since the recent operations commenced, for reports embracing their operations between the time of the attack above referred to and the time of their assignment to your command.

He wishes to have these before the army is disperged, that he may have some data on which to base his own report.

Very respectfully your obedient servant,
(Signed) W. H. Taylor, Assistant Adjutant-General.
Official: LATROBE, A. A. - G.
MAJOR-GENERAL G. E. PICKETT, Commanding.[529]

The next day, April 11, Lee began to receive reports from his subordinates. Most of them did not comment on the surrender. W. H. Stevens, the chief engineer, confirmed Lee's opinion about the necessity of surrendering and said that to have "attempted to cut a passage would have resulted in a frightful loss of life, giving no results at all commensurate with such a loss."[530]

In his report, W. N. Pendleton, the general chief of artillery, emphasized that the "conviction had become established in the minds of a large majority of our best officers and men that the army, in its extremely reduced state, could not be extricated from its perilous condition . . . unless with frightful bloodshed . . . . In view of these convictions, known of in part by him, and of all the facts before his own mind, the commanding general, before the battle had raged extensively, made arrangements for arresting the hostilities."[531] Here Pendleton made it plain that Lee was not alone in his decision to surrender the army and that he was supported by "a large majority of our best officers and men."

Writing in 1885, T. L. Rosser tried to deny that the officers and men in the Army of Northern Virginia were in favor of the surrender. He said that he felt the only answer which a surrender proposition "could receive would be that of the Old Guard: We can die, but we cannot surrender! If the army had been consulted this would have been its answer."[532]

As will be noted later, General Lee commented on the way his men straggled from the ranks on the retreat from Petersburg and told President Jefferson Davis that he could judge from this "the state of feeling which existed in the army . . .". Judging by the actions of the men in the Army of Northern Virginia, it must be presumed that most of them did agree with General Lee that the time for surrender had come.

J. L. Chamberlain said that he talked with several Confederate generals at Appomattox and that the impression he received from all of them was that they were ready to accept for themselves and for the Confederacy any fate which the United States government should dictate.[533]

In General R. E. Lee's report to President Jefferson Davis in regard to the surrender, he took the full responsibility for the surrender and did not mention that his decision had the support of the majority of his officers. He said: "I requested a suspension of hostilities" . . . "the interview which occurred with General Grant in compliance with my request" . . . "I surrendered that portion of the army of Northern Virginia which was on the field" . . . "I deemed this course the best under all the circumstances" . . . "the men, deprived of food and sleep for many days, were worn out and exhausted."[534]

A few days later, another communication from Lee to Davis had a somewhat different tone. In a letter to President Jefferson Davis, written on April 20, General Lee stressed the straggling of his army. He said: "At the commencement of the withdrawal of the army from the lines on the night of the 2d, it began to disintegrate, and straggling from the ranks increased up to the surrender on the 9th. On that day, as previously reported, there were only seven-thousand eight-hundred and ninety-two (7,892) effective infantry. During the night, when the surrender became known, more than ten thousand men came in, as reported to me by the Commissary of the Army. . . . I have given these details that Your Excellency might know the state of feeling which existed in the army, and judge of that in the country. . . . To save useless effusion of blood, I should recommend measures be taken for suspension of hostilities and the restoration of peace."[535]

While Lee must have been disappointed by the conduct of many of his men, this seems to be the closest he ever came to criticizing their behaviour. He apparently did not discuss the surrender in any of his postwar letters or writings. He wrote Colonel W. H. Taylor on July 31, 1865, that he wanted to collect data for a history of the campaigns in Virginia in order that "the bravery and devotion of the Army of Northern Virginia shall be correctly transmitted to posterity."[536] The tone of this letter was quite different from that in his letter of April 20. Here he spoke of "the worth of its (the Army of Northern Virginia) noble officers and soldiers" and evidently was ready to extend high praise to his old troopers. As is well known, he never succeeded in carrying out his desire to write a history of the Army of Northern Virginia.

THE SURRENDER IN THE REPORTS OF UNION OFFICERS

Like the Confederate officers, not many Union officers made extensive comments on the surrender in their official reports. Most of them were content merely to mention the surrender and to say that their units were present when this notable event took place.

A few Union officers did express their feelings on this subject, and some of their comments will be noted at this point.

Colonel T. F. McCoy, of the 107th Pennsylvania Infantry Regiment, closed his report with a fervent expression of gratitude to Almighty God.

> In closing this, which will doubtless be the last and final report of battles for this regiment, I would express my gratitude to a kind and ever merciful Providence that He has permitted us to pass through the many exposures, hardships, and great perils of this last great and closing campaign of an unprecedented war with comparatively so little sacrifice of life and blood, and that the lives and the health of so many brave officers and men of the regiment have been preserved, under the shield of His almighty power during the past three eventful years, to return to their homes to dwell in peace and rejoice over violated laws vindicated, a righteous Government preserved, the Union restored, and the old flag re-established with more than its original power, beauty, and significance, in some honorable degree through their instrumentality.[537]

A number of officers mentioned the joy and enthusiasm with which the news of the surrender was received by the men in their commands. Major General H. G. Wright said:

> Soon after halting official intelligence of the surrender of General Lee's forces was announced to the army, and was received with great enthusiasm by the soldiers, who looked upon this as the result of all their privations, and as the virtual ending of the struggle which had convulsed the country for four years, in which they had willingly risked their lives and fortunes.[538]

Major General George G. Meade hardly mentioned the surrender in his report. He simply said: "Nothing could exceed the cheerfulness with which all submitted to fatigue and privations to secure the coveted prize

-the capture of the Army of Northern Virginia."[539] Although any interpretation based upon silence does not have a strong basis, it is possible to see in Meade's statement his lack of enthusiasm for the praise which had been given to other commands, especially the Union cavalry forces.

Sheridan apparently did not comment on the surrender in any of his official reports. In his *Personal Memoirs,* however, he made it plain that he was willing to give Grant the credit for bringing about the surrender, saying that Grant "was the steadfast centre about and on which everything else turned."[540]

Sheridan, without mentioning their names, criticized both McClellan and Meade for failing to follow up the battles of Antietam and Gettysburg and said that "after each of these battles Lee was left unmolested till he had a chance to recuperate."[541]

One of the most eloquent passages in the official reports of Union officers is a paragraph in the report of Brevet Major General Wesley Merritt. From the standpoint of literary style and beauty it probably excels even the purpose passages of J. L. Chamberlain.

> It is impossible to overestimate the value of this day's work. The enemy's supplies were taken, as it were, out of their mouths. A strong force, they knew not how strong, was posted along their line of retreat at a point where they did not expect opposition. Night was upon them; tired, dispirited, and starving they lay at our feet. Their bravest soldiers, their hardiest men, gave way when they heard the noise of battle far in the rear, and the night of despair fell with the night of the 8th of April darkly and terribly on the Army of Northern Virginia.[542]

Brigadier General J. L. Chamberlain later wrote the classic description of the surrender in his *The Passing of the Armies.* His official report was written in a matter-of-fact manner and did not even mention the surrender.

Major General John Gibbon praised his troops for their long and rapid marches in the attempt to get ahead of Lee's retreating army: "By their rapid marching they twice succeeded in throwing themselves across the path of Lee's retreating forces, and by their firm stand there aided materially in the grand final result of the campaign."[543]

The First Division of the XXIV Union Army Corps evidently felt that this division did not receive enough credit for blocking the Lynchburg road on the morning of April 9. While he did it in a rather modest manner, Brigadier General R. S. Foster, commanding the First Division, made it very clear that he thought his division should receive credit for this achievement.

> I do not consider it egotistical to say, to this division is due

> the credit of preventing the enemy from gaining possession of the Lynchburg road (their only line of retreat), and of being among those who struck the last blow against the Army of Northern Virginia.[544]

Lieutenant General U. S. Grant endeavored to place all the Union troops on an equal footing and said that "all have a proud record." His words were a virtual plea for the men he commanded to rise above sectional jealousies.

> It has been my fortune to see the armies of both the West and the East fight battles, and from what I have seen I know there is no difference in their fighting qualities. All that is possible for men to do in battle they have done. The Western armies commenced their battles in the Mississippi Valley, and received the final surrender of the principal army opposed to them in North Carolina. The armies of the East commenced their battles on the river from which the Army of the Potomac derived its name, and received the final surrender of their old antagonist at Appomattox Court-House, Va. The splendid achievements of each have nationalized our victories, removed all sectional jealousies (of which we have unfortunately experienced too much), and the cause of crimination and recrimination that might have followed had either section failed in its duty. All have a proud record, and all sections can well congratulate themselves and each other for having done their full share in restoring the supremacy of law over every foot of territory belonging to the United States. Let them hope for perpetual peace and harmony with that enemy whose manhood, however mistaken the cause, drew forth such herculean deeds of valor.[545]

FRATERNIZING AMONG THE TROOPS

Although it was officially forbidden,[546] there was quite a bit of fraternizing among the Union and Confederate troops at Appomattox as soon as the surrender was announced.

Picket lines were established, and the pickets were supposed to prevent any fraternizing, but there was still much visiting back and forth between the lines. This had always gone on during the war years. Men frequently swapped coffee and tobacco and drank from the same spring after a battle.

Charles E. Dunn, a private in the 20th Maine Regiment, said that there was a great deal of trading on the night of April 9 and that the picket lines were practically deserted.

> The two picket lines were within speaking distance, and we were on speaking terms with the "Johnnies" at once. There was nothing that resembled guard duty that night. It resembled a picnic rather than a picket line. They like ourselves were glad the war was over. We exchanged knicknacks with them, and were reminded of the days when at school we swapped jews-harps for old wooden toothed combs. The articles we exchanged that night were about the same value. . . . It came on to rain about midnight, and the camp fires of the Fifth Corps on the hillside half a mile away looked mighty attractive. To our Johnnie friends (not our enemies now) the camp fires of their army in the valley below had the same attraction. After a short conference both sides voted unanimously to desert the picket line and go to camp.[547]

Confederate reports spoke of the fraternizing and said that Federal officers and men were very courteous when they came into the Confederate lines.

> During Sunday and Monday, a large number of Federal soldiers and officers visited our camps and looked curiously on our command, but there was nothing like exultation, no shouting for joy, and no word uttered that could add to the mortification already sustained. On the contrary, every symptom of respect was manifested, and the Southern army was praised for the brave and noble manner in which it had defended our cause. . . .
>
> All the Federals spoke of Gen. Lee in terms of unbounded praise. The remark was frequently made, "he would receive as many cheers in going down our lines as General Grant himself."[548]

It appears that Union soldiers were more anxious to visit the Confederate camps than vice versa. Hunger and fatique undoubtedly dulled the curiosity of many a man of the Confederate army. One Confederate spoke of the sufferings being "mercifully deadened by a stupor" at the time of the surrender.[549]

As was to be expected on such an occasion, not all the contacts between the members of the two armies were pleasant. It was hard for some of the Confederates to hide their bitterness and resentment, and some frankly expressed their hatred for the Union.

Brigadier General J. L. Chamberlain approached Brigadier General Henry A. Wise with a polite expresson of hope for future good will between the North and South. Wise testily replied, "There is a rancor in our hearts which you little dream of. We hate you, sir".[550]

Captain W. N. McDonald of Mahone's Division said that a Union colonel spoke to a group of Confederates and told them that the North loved the South and that the next President of the United States would be General Lee.

> Finally he said, "We are all a band of brothers now," and seemed to pause for a reply. A grim, battlescarred veteran responded in audible tones and with an oath, "if I had you out in the woods by yourself I'd brother you."[551]

General Lee had been afraid of unpleasant encounters between the men of the two armies and had given that as his reason for requesting that they be kept separate.[552]

SOUVENIRS FROM THE McLEAN HOUSE

A craze for souvenirs from the McLean House seemed to come over the Union officers at Appomattox Court House. As soon as the surrender letters were made out, and Grant and Lee had departed, offers were made to Major Wilmer S. McLean for the pieces of furniture in the surrender room.

It is said that members of the McLean family denied that any articles were sold and claimed that Union officers looted the house.[553] One of Custer's biographers, on the other hand, said that McLean definitely "offered to sell the furniture."[554]

On this point, it appears that McLean sold some pieces, and refused to sell other pieces. Some of the pieces which he refused to sell were evidently carried away without his consent.

Sheridan is reported to have paid twenty dollars in gold for the small oval-topped table. He then presented the table to Custer as a gift for Mrs. Custer. Along with the table he sent the following message:

> My dear Madam - I respectfully present to you the small writing-table on which the conditions of the surrender of the Confederate Army of Northern Virginia were written by Lt. General Grant - and permit me to say, Madam, that there is scarcely an individual in our service who has contributed more to bring this about than your very gallant husband.[555]

Someone spoke to Mrs. Custer about this gift and remarked that Sheridan was a tender-hearted man to think of a woman under such circumstances. Mrs. Custer replied that she thought she deserved the table "for Sheridan frequently asserted that my husband was the only one who had not been spoiled by marriage."[556]

E. O. C. Ord bought the other table in the room. Horace Porter said that Ord later presented the table to Mrs. U. S. Grant, who modestly declined it and insisted that Mrs. Ord should become its possessor.[557]

Sylvanus Cadwallader said that there has been much "contention between the families of these distinguished officers, as to which of them owned the celebrated table used on the day of the surrender."[558]

The table which Custer carried away is now in the Smithsonian Institution in Washington. The other is in possession of the Chicago Historical Society.

Sylvanus Cadwallader said that two cavalry officers seized the chairs which Grant and Lee had occupied and carried them off when McLean indignantly threw their "greenbacks" on the floor. Sometime later, a cavalryman came back and thrust a ten dollar bill into McLean's hands, saying, "This is for the Major's chair." A diligent search was made for the chairs, and the officers who confiscated them, but neither could be found.[559]

Horace Porter gave the following report in regard to the individuals who carried away souvenirs:

> General Sharpe paid ten dollars for the pair of brass candlesticks; Colonel Sheridan, the Generals' brother, secured the stone inkstand; and General Capehart the chair in which Grant sat, which he gave not long before his death to Captain Wilmon W. Blackmar of Boston. Captain O'Farrell of Hartford became the possessor of the chair in which Lee sat. A child's doll was found in the room, which the younger officers tossed from one to the other, and call the "silent witness." This toy was taken possession of by Colonel Moore of Sheridan's staff, and is now owned by his son. Bargains were at once struck for nearly all the articles in the room; and it is even said that some momentos were carried off for which no coin of the republic was over exchanged. The sofa remains in possession of Mrs. Spillman, Mr. McLean's daughter, who now lives in Camden, West Virginia. Colonel Marshall presented the boxwood inkstand to Mr. Blanchard of Baltimore. Of the three impressions of the terms of surrender made in General Grant's manifold writer, the first and third are believed to have been accidentally destroyed. No trace of them has since been discovered; the second is in the possession of the New York Commandery of the Military Order of the Loyal Legion, which purchased it recently from the widow of General Parker.[560]

Cadwallader said that the cane splits in cane bottomed chairs were broken into small pieces and distributed as souvenirs. Haircloth upholstery was cut into strips and patches and carried away.[561]

Gibbon mentioned that he carried his own table into the surrender room for the signing of the formal terms of surrender by the six generals on the night of April 10.[562] Since he did not say anything about the other furniture in the room, it appears that Cadwallader's statement about the destruction of furniture in the surrender room needs verification from other sources. No other accounts with these details were discovered during the research carried on for this study.

THE APPLE TREE AND THE SURRENDER

Although it has no factual basis, and is easily disproved, the story of the "surrender under the apple tree" has been one of the most persistent of all the numerous Appomattox legends. Often denied, it is still circulated and believed in many circles.

E. P. Alexander gave what appears to be a realistic account of how the apple tree came to be connected with General Lee on the morning of April 9.

> After some delay Lee had received a message from Grant that he had left the rear of our army and was passing along his own lines around to our front. Lee accordingly returned, and passing through our line of battle, dismounted close in front, in an apple-orchard, near a house said to be the home of Sweeny, celebrated as a minstrel and banjo-player before the war. Here he was left standing alone for a few minutes, having sent his staff off on various errands, and as he expressed a desire to sit down, I had some rails brought from a fence near by, and a seat piled for him under one of the apple-trees, a short distance from the road. He sat there for perhaps two hours, close in front of Longstreet's line of battle, until Babcock of Grant's staff came from Appomattox to escort him there to meet Grant.
>
> I made my bivouac in that orchard that night. Relic-hunters had already begun to cut limbs from the apple-tree under which Lee sat, and within twenty-four hours it was literally dug up by the roots, and not a clip of it was left. I have always regretted since that I did not appreciate how I should come to value some memorial of the event, and myself secure a piece of the tree as a momento; for I have since tried in vain to get a piece even as big as a tooth-pick. I think it was carried off entirely by Confederates who, standing in our last line of battle, saw Lee sitting under the tree awaiting Grant's messenger.[563] I have never even heard of more than one piece of it since. One of my sisters, "refugeeing" through Carolina, first heard the story of the surrender from a Texan who had been present and seen Lee

under the tree, and had cut himself a walking-stick from it, and was now footing it for home.[564]

Colonel Charles Marshall gave substantially the same account. He said that General Lee had been in the saddle all night and was so very much fatigued that he lay down and went to sleep under the apple tree.[565]

Another observer described General Lee as "seated for a long time, with crossed arms and bowed head, immovable as stone, on a broken rail, under an old apple tree, whose scanty foliage and feeble bloom were in keeping with the general dilapidation of the homestead in its rear, which I learned was the birthplace of Sweeny, the famous banjo player."[566]

Lt. General Grant denied on several occasions that he had any meeting with General Lee under the apple tree. In his *Memoirs* he said:

> Before stating what took place between General Lee and myself I will give all there is of the story and of the famous apple-tree.
>
> Wars produce many stories of fiction, some of which are told until they are believed to be true. The war of the rebellion was no exception to this rule, and the story of the apple-tree is one of those fictions based on a slight foundation of fact. As I have said, there was an apple-orchard on the side of the hill occupied by the Confederate forces. Running diagonally up the hill was a wagon-road, which at one point ran very near one of the trees, so that the wheels of vehicles had on that side cut off the roots of this tree, leaving only a little embankment. General Babcock, of my staff, reported to me that when he first met General Lee he was sitting upon this embankment with his feet in the road below and his back resting against the tree. The story had no other foundation than that. Like many other stories, it would be very good if it were only true.[567]

As pointed out by Grant, the apple tree did have some connection with the surrender proceedings. It was the spot where General Lee waited until he was contacted by Babcock, and this was apparently enough to set off the rumor among the troops that the surrender actually took place under the apple tree.

Many of the soldiers who were at Appomattox, and who saw what happened at the apple tree, somehow gained the impression that the surrender took place there. J. L. Smith of the 118th Pennsylvania Volunteers said that his regiment was "lying near the hill" close to the apple tree and that he "was early at the spot and secured a piece of the tree." He wrote to Grant about it because "these denials are having a run through the papers tending to bring my relic into disrepute, and my friends tell me that the occurrence did not take place under the tree, I ask you, general, to set the matter right."[568]

At the time of the surrender, the apple tree story was printed in many newspapers, especially in the South, and was firmly planted in the minds of many people as the solid truth. An unknown newspaper correspondent sent out the following story:

> Soon after the return of General Custar (sic) to his lines, General Grant, accompanied by his staff, rode to the headquarters of Gen. Lee, which were under an apple tree, near the road. The interview is described as exceedingly impressive.[569]

Did this writer deliberately distort the facts in order to present the surrender in a more favorable light from a Southern point of view? Perhaps Grant believed this, because he pointed out that "Lee was conducted to McLean's house, within our lines, before I got up."[570] The words "within our lines" may have some significance. Grant might have become tired of hearing people say that he went to meet Lee at the apple tree, which was within the Confederate lines, when Lee actually went to meet Grant at the McLean House, which was within the Union lines.

After the Civil War ended, Southern writers often accused Northern authors of trying to perpetuate the apple tree myth and of giving a false picture of what actually happened at Appomattox. One Southerner spoke of the apple tree story as "a falsehood that promises to have a permanent existence in Northern books."[571] It may be true, however, that the apple tree story was given its strongest lease on life by Southern newspapers in 1865.

An article appeared in the Lynchburg *News* on June 11, 1924, with the title: "Renew Discussion of Story that Lee Surrendered Under Old Apple Tree." It was stated that the Appomattox Chapter of the U. D. C. had received a letter suggesting that "permanent preservation of the historical apple tree be made. It was reported to them, says the letter, that the old tree was standing unprotected and that a tree of such history ought to be preserved as a worthy memorial to the Confederate general." The writer of the article then went on to discount the story of the surrender under the apple tree.

The Confederate Museum in Columbia, South Carolina, has a piece of wood in one of its exhibits which is supposed to be a portion of the apple tree. It would be difficult, to say the least, to establish the authenticity of such relics.

Following the war, "apple tree jewelry" became a popular item, and a New York jewelry firm presented a set of such jewelry to Mrs. U. S. Grant. It was said: "The wood used in this set was cut from the apple tree under which General Grant's officers met General Lee on the morning of the surrender, April 9, 1865."[572]

Thomas G. Jones said:

> This apple tree was in an orchard fully half a mile from the Court House. Nothing occurred near it nor under it; and yet out of this was made the story of Lee's surrendering under an apple tree, and the whole orchard was cut down to supply "pieces of the apple tree under which Gen. Lee surrendered" to curiosity hunters and relic worshippers. Hundreds of thousands of dollars worth of jewelry were made out of this same small tree.[573]

THE SWORD OF GENERAL R. E. LEE

One of the best-known legends connected with the surrender of the Army of Northern Virginia is the story that General R. E. Lee tendered his sword to Lieutenant-General Grant as a token of the surrender but that it was graciously and magnanimously returned to him by the Union commander.

Grant denied that there was any truth in the story and said that it was the purest romance. He stated:

> The much-talked-of surrendering of Lee's sword and my handing it back, this and much more that has been said about it is the purest romance. The word "sword" or "side-arms" was not mentioned by either of us until I wrote it in the terms.[574]

A denial by General Lee was quoted by J. W. Jones. It must be admitted that this denial has something less than an authentic sound, especially because of its belligerent tones.

> "General Grant returned you your sword, did he not, general?" one of the company asked. The old hero, straightening himself up, replied, in most emphatic tones; "No, sir! he did not. He had no opportunity of doing so. I was determined that the side-arms of officers should be exempt by the terms of surrender, and of course I did not offer him mine. All that was said about swords was that General Grant apologized to me for not wearing his own sword, saying that it had gone off in his baggage, and he had been unable to get it in time."[575]

Whether or not General Lee denied the sword story is of little importance, because the denial by Grant is quite sufficient to destroy its validity. Freeman did not consider the story worthy of any space in the text of his biography of Lee and relegated it to a foot-note.[576]

Some Southern writers have believed that the sword story was invented by Northern artists and authors in an attempt to set forth Grant's magnanimity in an even more favorable light. J. W. Jones held this opinion. He said:

> This (Lee's denial of the story) spoils a great deal of rhetoric about "Grant's magnanimity in returning Lee's sword," and renders as absurd as it is false the attempt of Northern artists to put the scene on canvas or into statuary. Even General Grant's connivance at this so-called "historic scene" will not have it when the world knows that R. E. Lee said that *nothing of the sort occurred.*[577]

Like the story of the surrender under the apple tree, however, it seems that the story about Grant's returning the sword of Lee probably obtained its first lease on life through the story of the surrender which appeared in many Southern newspapers.[578] After saying that Grant went to meet Lee under an apple tree, this story continued as follows:

> After the "salutary formalities, which doubtless were brief and business-like — General Lee tendered his sword to General Grant in token of surrender. That officer, however, with a courtesy for which we must accord him due respect, declined to receive it, or receiving, declined to retain it, and accompanied its return with substantially the following remark: Gen. Lee keep the sword. You have won it by your gallantry. You have not been whipped, but overpowered, and I cannot receive it as a token of surrender from so brave a man." The reply of Gen. Lee, we do not know. But Grant and himself are said to have been deeply affected by the solemnity of the occasion and to have shed tears. The scene occurred between ten and eleven o'clock a.m.

As Grant declared, anyone who is familiar with the events at Appomattox Court House can readily see that this story was "the purest romance" and the product of some writer's vivid imagination. This unknown scribbler, who hardly deserves the title of newspaper correspondent, must nevertheless be given credit for helping to launch one of the most persistent legends in American history.

Instead of glorifying Grant, as Jones seemed to think, it appears that the story about Lee's sword was originally intended to magnify the gallantry and bravery of Lee. The words which the writer put into the mouth of Grant undoubtedly delighted many sad hearts throughout the Confederacy.

Horace Porter, Badeau, Cadwallader, and even Grant himself were all mistaken about the origin of Lee's sword. It was not, as Porter said, "the sword that had been presented to him by the State of Virginia."[579] Neither did it have a "hilt studded with jewels."[580]

Fitzhugh Lee gave the following description of the sword carried by R. E. Lee at his surrender conference with Grant:

> The handle of this sword is white, with a lion's head at the top and wrapped with gilt wire (not studded with jewels, as has been published), with gilt guard, the scabbard of blue steel with gilt trimmings. Where the rings are attached, on one side of the blade, are the words, "General Robert E. Lee, from a Marylander, 1863"; on the other "Aide toi et Diew t'aiders." This sword is in the possession of General G. W. C. Lee, son of General Lee, and the President of Washington and Lee University at Lexington, Va.[581]

Lee's surrender sword is now on display at the Confederate Museum in Richmond.[582]

A picture of this sword is in Freeman's *R. E. Lee,* Volume IV, facing page 166.

After the war, a story was circulated that Brig. Gen. J. L. Chamberlain claimed that he received Lee's sword on April 12. Chamberlain said that he never made such a claim and that he "never did receive that sword."[583]

HORACE PORTER'S ACCOUNT OF THE SURRENDER

One of the best-known accounts of the surrender at Appomattox Court House is the narrative written by General Horace Porter, which was published in *Battles and Leaders,* Volume IV, pages 729-746, under the title, "The Surrender at Appomattox Court House."

This material was later included in *Campaigning With Grant.* New York: The Century Co., 1897. It was given here in a slightly expanded form and included more details about the souvenirs which were carried away from the McLean House.

In *The Century Illustrated Monthly Magazine* for April, 1902, the editor proudly stated that General Horace Porter "has given to the world the most detailed account of the conversation" between Grant and Lee.[584] He also implied that it was the most trustworthy account.

Porter's *Campaigning With Grant* was recently published by the Indiana University Press, with an introduction and notes by Wayne C. Temple.[585] This edition of Porter's work contains a foreword, written by Robert H. Ferrell and approved by Kenneth P. Williams, which stoutly defends the general trustworthiness of Porter's account.

> What, then, of the general trustworthiness of Porter's *Campaigning with Grant?* This book, like the memoirs of Cadwallader, was written many years after the events it describes. Is it a reliable guide?

> Two factors point to the unimpeachable honesty of Horace Porter's account. For one thing, Porter kept voluminous notes of his association with Grant, and used them to write his memoirs published in 1897. These notes, one should add, have unfortunately disappeared, and are not in the Horace Porter Papers in the Library of Congress; there seems to be no doubt of their existence at the time Porter wrote his book, but thereafter they vanished. Needless to add, if they could be discovered they would be of prime historical importance, containing among other things the only eyewitness account of the Appomattox surrender.
>
> A second reason for the reliability of Porter's book is that its author had no special reason to write the volume, apart from a desire to set down the facts of his association with Grant. By the turn of the century, when the book appeared, Porter was one of the best known men in America. There was no need for him to increase his reputation by abridging history.[586]

Wayne C. Temple said that "Porter's account of the surrender of Lee is certainly much more accurate than that of Sylvanus Cadwallader."[587]

Porter's account seems to be highly regarded by virtually all Civil War historians and is quite frequently quoted. It is generally looked upon as a trustworthy, first-hand account of what transpired between Grant and Lee on the memorial day of April 9, 1865.

Although Freeman questioned several of Porter's statements in the foot-notes of his biography of General Lee,[588] he did not indicate that he had any doubts about the general authenticity of Porter's work. Like many other Civil War historians, Freeman was evidently inclined to overvalue Porter's account and did not scrutinize it as carefully as he should have.

However, a close examination of Porter's narrative reveals that it contains a large number of errors and that its general trustworthiness is therefore highly questionable.

Some of Porter's statements were simply not in accordance with known facts. For example, he said in regard to the McLean House.

> The house had a comfortable wooden porch with seven steps leading up to it. A hall ran through the middle from front to back, and on each side was a room having two windows, one in front and one in rear. Each room had two doors opening into the hall.[589]

There are eight steps leading up to the porch of the McLean House instead of seven, and the rooms opening into the downstairs hall have only one door instead of two.

Porter said that Lee's sword had a hilt studded with jewels.[590] The surrender sword in the Confederate Museum in Richmond has a hilt wrapped with gilt wire and is not studded with jewels.

When Lee and Babcock started to ride toward the village of Appomattox Court House, Porter said that they were accompanied by Colonel Charles Marshall and an orderly. He failed to mention Babcock's orderly.[591]

Porter was mistaken in saying that the entire party went forward together and that General Lee selected the meeting place for the surrender conference.[592] Marshall said that he rode forward with an orderly to do this.[593]

Porter said that the house which Wilmer McLean first showed them was "meagerly furnished"[594] but Marshall said that it had no furniture at all.[595].

Porter stated that Grant was alone when he first entered the surrender room at the McLean House and that the members of his staff and other Union officers remained outside until Grant sent Babcock to give them an invitation to enter the house. Porter said that the officers remained in the room, and were able to hear the conversation between the two generals, but were not introduced to Lee until the surrender letters were being copied.[596]

Sheridan gave a different version. He said that the Union officers entered the room, were presented to General Lee, and then some withdrew until the two generals had come to an agreement on the terms of the surrender. He did not say that he heard any of the preliminary conversation. When Babcock invited them to come in again, he said: "The surrender has been made; you can come in again."[597]

Like Sheridan, Marshall said that Grant introduced his officers to Lee at the very beginning of the conference.[598]

According to Porter, Grant opened his conversation with Lee by talking about the time he and Lee had served together in Mexico. He is said to have remarked that he remembered Lee very well, while Lee declared that he could not recall a single feature of Grant.[599]

This was definitely contradicted by Marshall, who said: "He walked up to General Lee and Lee recognized him at once.[600] Grant himself said that Lee told him that "he remembered me very well in the old army."[601]

Porter said that Wilmer McLean's ink "had disappeared" and that "Colonel Marshall now came to the rescue, and pulled out of his pocket a small box-wood inkstand, which was put at Parker's service."[602] Marshall, on the other hand, stated that he had the inkstand in a little satchel that he had at his side.[603]

One of Porter's famous conjectures was that Lee mistook Ely S. Parker, a full-blooded Indian on Grant's staff, for a Negro and "was struck with astonishment to find that the commander of the Union armies had one of that race on his personal staff."[604]

This was an inference that Parker indignantly denied. Parker said that Lee stared at him for a moment and then extended his hand and said, "I am glad to see one real American here."

Parker stated that he shook Lee's hand and replied, "We are all Americans."[605]

Porter said that Lee made some comments about expecting to receive several trainloads of rations from Lynchburg, which indicated that he did not know that Sheridan had captured these trains the night before at Appomattox Station.[606] It is likely, however, that Pendleton reported the presence of the trains at Appomattox Station and advised Lee of their probable capture when he talked with the Confederate commander at 1 A.M. on April 9. It seems proper to infer this from Pendleton's report in the *Official Records*.[607]

Porter stated that Lee told Grant, in response to Grant's question, that he did not know how many men were in his command on the day of the surrender.[608] Grant himself said that Lee replied, "About twenty-five thousand."[609] Freeman said in regard to Porter's statement that the evidence was "against its literal accuracy."[610]

When Grant apologized to Lee for not having on a sword, Porter wrote: "I am in the habit of wearing mine most of the time," remarked Lee; "I wear it invariably when I am among my troops, moving about through the army."[611]

Freeman wisely commented: "There was, however, some misunderstanding here as Lee rarely wore a sword."[612]

Porter's statement that Lee shook Grant's hand and bade him farewell a little before 4 o'clock seems to make the hour of Lee's departure entirely too late. If, as Porter said, the surrender conference got underway at 1:30 P.M., and concluded at 4:00 P.M. Grant and Lee would have talked for two and a half hours.[613]

Marshall said that the conference was brief and lasted approximately one hour.[614]

Porter's description of the final farewell between Grant and Lee in the yard of the McLean House, after which Grant "then mounted and started for the headquarters camp",[615] does not seem to fit the facts. Henry Heth said that he spent half an hour talking with Grant on the day of the surrender, and it seems that this conversation must have taken place in the McLean House following the surrender conference.[616]

Also, if Grant left the McLean House immediately after Lee departed, why was his dispatch to Washington, which was written by the roadside between the McLean House and his headquarters, not sent off until 4:30 P.M.?[617]

It is known that Grant smoked a cigar during the entire surrender conference.[618] Freeman noted that Grant "puffed furiously" but for some strange reason substituted a pipe for Grant's cigar.[619] It seems even stranger that Porter, who mentioned so many other small details, should have failed to include Grant's cigar in his narrative.

Porter's statement that Lee rode at a gallop to meet Grant on April 10[620] was disputed by some of the Confederates who were on the picket line.[621]

Freeman questioned Porter's report of the conversation between Grant and Lee on April 10 and said that his account "seems a bit embroidered with time, and it has the emphasis in the wrong place."[622]

Many other misstatements in Porter's account have not been mentioned in this survey, but the errors noted are regarded as being sufficient to prove that his account of the surrender should be used with considerable caution and that his statements should be verified from other sources.

CONCLUSIONS

The research carried on for this study has demonstrated again how essential it is to emply extreme caution in evaluating and using all source material, whether published or unpublished, in regard to the events connected with the surrender of the Army of Northern Virginia.

Various versions, not only by different authors, but also by the same author, should always be diligently compared, because errors of fact, misstatements, and false assumptions are often found in highly-regarded narratives and in the writings of trusted authors. A conspicuous example of this is the account of the surrender by General Horace Porter. Although frequently quoted by outstanding historians, this account seems to be very untrustworthy at a number of points. The accounts by Gordon, Longstreet, and others are likewise often inaccurate.

In spite of conflicting statements, it has been possible to arrive at reasonably accurate conclusions in regard to most of the disputed points connected with the surrender proceedings. On the questions where it is still impossible to make a final judgment, because of the lack of sufficient evidence, it is believed that continued research will eventually succeed in solving most of these problems. It is thought that we now have a fairly dependable picture of one of the greatest events in American history.

ACKNOWLEDGEMENTS

The preparation of this study was made much easier by the assistance of Supt. T. F. Norris, Jr., and Park Historian James Haskett. They made available the material in the files at Appomattox Court House National Historical Park and gave a number of valuable suggestions.

While the library staffs at many places were very helpful, it is felt that a special word of appreciation should be given to the staff of the Jones Memorial Library, Lynchburg, Virginia. This library has an outstanding collection of Civil War material. Many books not in the library were kindly secured through the interlibrary loan system.

Among the many collections of material which were found useful, the following are singled out for special mention: University of Virginia Library; Virginia Historical Society Library; the Library of Congress; the South Carolinia Library; University of South Carolina; Southern Historical Collection, University of North Carolina; Duke University Library; the American Jewish Archives, Cincinnati, Ohio; the Department of Archives and History, State of Alabama, Montgomery, Alabama; the Department of Archives and History, United States Military Academy, West Point, New York.

Gratitude is expressed to C. E. Dornbusch, Civil War bibliographer at the New York Public Library, for his unfailing kindness and promptness in answering all inquiries.

CITATIONS

1. Grant, U. S., *Personal Memoirs of U. S. Grant.* Vol. II. New York: The Century Co., 1903, pp. 332-333.
2. Q. R., XLVI, Pt. 1, p. 56
3. Gibbon, John, "Personal Recollections of Appomattox," *The Century Illustrated Monthly Magazine,* LXIII (1902) 937.
4. Porter, Horace, "The Surrender at Appomattox Court House." *Battles and Leaders of the Civil War,* edited by R. U. Johnson and C. C. Buel, Vol. IV. New York: The Century Company, 1888, p. 730.
5. Schaff, Morris, *The Sunset of the Confederacy.* Boston: John W. Luce and Co., 1912, pp. 137-138.
6. The text of this letter is also given in *O. R.* XLVI, Pt. 1, p. 56, but the complete heading, salutation, and conclusion are not printed in this version.

   Freeman, D. S., *R. E. Lee,* Vol. IV. New York: Charles Scribner's Sons, 1935, p. 103, has a misprint in the text of this letter. "Results" should be singular instead of plural. This book cited hereafter as *Lee,* IV.
7. Freeman, D. S., *Lee* IV, p. 106, mistakenly refers to Williams as Grant's inspector general.
8. *O. R.,* XLVI, Pt. 3, p. 626.
9. Ibid., 627
10. Sorrel, G. M., *Recollections of a Confederate Staff Officer.* New York and Washington: The Neal Publishing Co., 1905, p. 308.
11. *Ibid.,* 310. Other details are in Schaff, *op. cit.,* 149-153.
12. Freeman said that the time was "about half-past nine or perhaps a little later". *Lee,* IV, p. 103. It does not seem that the time could have been as early as 9:30. Perry said that the flag of truce appeared about 9:00. Permission then had to be obtained from division headquarters to answer it. Perry walked out beyond the picket lines, where he talked with some of the Federal wounded, and then went on for his interview with Williams. After he returned with Grant's letter, it took another twenty minutes for it to be delivered to General Lee. All of these things could easily have taken a solid hour.
13. DePeyster, J. W., "Andrew Atkinson Humphreys," *The Magazine of American History, XVI,* (1886), 366.
14. *Lee, IV,* p. 103, not 62.
15. Longstreet, J., *From Manassas to Appomattox.* Philadelphia: J. B. Lippincott Co., 1903, p. 619.
16. *Lee, IV,* pp. 105-106.
17. Maurice, Frederick, ed., *An Aide-De-Camp of Lee being the Papers of Colonel Charles Marshall.* Boston: Little, Brown, and Co., 1927, p. 254. Freeman refers to Marshall's statement in a footnote, *Lee, IV, p. 106, note 2, but says that he considered the reference "not conclusive".*
18. *Lee,* IV, p. 112, note 28.
19. *Lee,* IV, p. 112.
20. Thomas B. F., ed., *Three Years with Grant. As Recalled by War Correspondent Sylvanus Cadwallader.* New York: Alfred A. Knopf, 1955, pp. 316-317.
21. Maurice, *op. cit.,* 255.
22. The text of this letter in *O. R.* XLVI, Pt. 3, p. 619, does not include the full conclusion. The original letter in the U. S. War Department shows that the original did have the full conclusion as given here.
23. Pendleton, W. N., "Personal Recollections of General Lee," *The Southern Magazine,* XV (1874), 633.
24. Porter, *op. cit.,* 730.
25. *Lee,* IV, p. 106.
26. Porter, *op. cit.,* 730.
27. *O. R.,* XLVI, Pt. 1, p. 56.
28. Morris Schaff said that Seth Williams did not leave Farmville with Grant's reply until "day had broken". Schaff, *op. cit.,* 169. Since Grant said that he replied immediately to Lee's letter, this indicates that the letter was not received until around daybreak. Elsewhere, however, Schaff says that Williams "did not reach Grant at Farmville till midnight.'" *Ibid.,* 153. Schaff might not have noticed this inconsistency in his account.
29. Grant, *op. cit.,* 334.
30. *O. R.,* XLVI, Pt. 1, p. 56.
31. *O. R.,* XLVI, Pt. 3, p. 64.
32. Schaff, *op. cit.,* 168.
33. Ibid., 168-169.
34. *O. R.,* XLVI, Pt. 3, p. 643.
35. Rosser, T. L., "Appomattox," The Philadelphia *Weekly Times,* April 5, 1885.
36. *O. R.,* XLVI, Pt. 3, p. 643.
37. *O. R.,* XLVI, Pt. 3, p. 640.
38. Alexander, E. P., *Military Memoirs of a Confederate.* New York: Charles Scribner's Sons, 1910, p. 601.
39. Humphreys, A. A., *The Virginia Campaign of '64 and '65.* New York: Charles Scribner's Sons, 1883, p. 392.
40. *Lee,* IV, p. 112.
41. Schaff says that it was during the morning. *Op. cit.,* 140. Freeman says that it was "the previous evening" before April 8. *Lee,* IV, p. 109.
42. Schaff thought that this "discouraging intelligence from the South" was the news of the capture of Selma, Alabama, on April 2, *Op. cit.,* 145.
43. Pendleton, W. N., "Personal Recollections of General Lee," *The Southern Magazine,* XV (1874), 633. Pendleton, an Episcopal minister, frequently repeated this as part of an address which he made to raise funds for the Memorial Church in Lexington, Virginia. *Ibid.,* 603, note.

44. Gordon, J. B., *Reminiscences of the Civil War.* New York: Charles Scribner's Sons, 1913, p. 433.
45. Longstreet, *op. cit.,* 620.
46. *Lee, IV,* p. 110.
47. Schaff, *op. cit.,* 143.
48. *Ibid.,* 143.
49. Cockrell, M. F., ed., *Gunner With Stonewall.* Jackson: McCowat-Mercer Press, 1957, p. 119.
50. Pendleton, *op. cit.,* 603-636.
51. Alexander, E. P., "General Lee at Appomattox," *The Southern Magazine,* XII (1873), 747-752.
52. In his Select Critical Bibliography, Freeman made the following comment about Longstreet's book: "Important but inaccurate." Lee, IV, p. 562.
53. Freeman also repeated Longstreet's statement that Pendleton asked him to approach General Lee. *Lee,* IV, p. 110.
54. Alexander, *Military Memoirs,* 600-601.
55. Taylor W. H., *General Lee, His Campaigns in Virginia 1861-1865.* Norfolk: Nasbaum Book and News Co., 1906, p. 283.
56. Text quoted from *Lee,* IV, p. 113. Most of the printed versions change the abbreviations. While this does not change the meaning, the exact wording seems to be preferable. Also see *O. R.* XLVI, Pt. 3, p. 641.
57. Alexander, *Military Memoirs,* 601.
58. Dowdey, Clifford, and Manarin, L. H. eds., *The Wartime Papers of R. E. Lee.* Boston: Little, Brown and Co., 1961, p. 897.
59. *O. R.,* XLVI, Pt. 3, p. 664.
60. Humphreys, *op. cit.,* 392.
61. *O. R.,* XLVI, Pt. 1, p. 1303.
62. Gordon, *op. cit.,* 435.
63. *O. R.,* XLVI, Pt. 1, p. 1303.
64. *Ibid.,* 1303.
65. *Ibid., 1304.*
66. *Lee,* IV, p. 115.
67. "March of the Army of the James," New York *Freeman's Journal and Catholic Register,* April 22, 1865.
68. *O. R.,* XLVI, Pt. 1, p. 1162.
69. Rosser, T. L., "Appomattox," The Philadelphia *Weekly Times,* April 5, 1885.
70. Account of Maj. Gen. Bryan Grimes in *Five Points in the Record of North Carolina in the Great War of 1861-5.* Goldsboro: Nash Brothers, 1904, pp. 60-63.
71. Gordon, *op. cit.,* 436-437.
72. Thomas, *op. cit.,* 319.
73. *Ibid.,* 320.
74. *O. R.,* XLVI, Pt. 3, p. 664.
75. *Ibid.,* 663. This letter was headed "Clifton House, Va." His letter to Lee must have also been written at the Clifton House.
76. *O. R.,* XLVI, Pt. 1, p. 57.
77. Thomas, *op. cit.,* 320-321.
78. McClellan, Carswell, *The Personal Memoirs and Military History of U. S. Grant versus The Record of the Army of the Potomac.* Boston and New York: Houghton, Mifflin and Co., 1887, pp. 268-270; McClellan, Carswell, *Notes on the Personal Memoirs of P. H. Sheridan.* St. Paul: Press of W. E. Banning, Jr., 1889, p. 76.
79. Pennypacker, I. R., "The American Colkitto," *The Pennsylvania Magazine of History and Biography,* LVII, (1933), 148, 151.
80. Agassiz, G. R., ed., *Meade's Headquarters 1863-1865. Boston: Massachusetts Historical Society, 1922, p. 358.*
81. Humphreys, A. A., *The Virginia Campaign of '64 and '65.* New York: Charles Scribner's Sons, 1883, p. 394.
82. Grant, *op. cit.,* 338.
83. Henry, R. S., *The Story of the Confederacy.* Garden City: Garden City Publishing Co., 1931. p. 465.
84. Sheridan, P. H., *Personal Memoirs of P. H. Sheridan.* Vol. II. New York: Charles L. Webster and Co., 1888, p. 199.
85. *O. R.,* XLVI, Pt. 3, p. 640. Grant sent a message to Sheridan from Farmville on April 8 which said: "I think Lee will surrender to-day." *Ibid.,* 652.
86. Thomas, *op. cit.,* 319-320.
87. Grant, *op. cit.,* 341.
88. Alexander, E. P., *Military Memoirs of a Confederate.* New York: Charles Scribner's Sons, 1910, p. 602.
89. Gordon, *op. cit.,* 438.
90. *Ibid.,* 438.
91. *Lee,* IV, p. 119.
92. Schaff, *op. cit.,* 227-228.
93. Gordon, *op. cit.,* 438.
94. *Ibid.,* 438.
95. Davis, Jefferson. *The Rise and Fall of the Confederate Government.* Vol. II. New York: D. Appleton and Co., 1881, p. 657.
96. Humphreys, *op. cit.* 392, and note 1.
97. *Lee* IV, p. 120, and note 24.

98. *Lee* IV, pp. 119-124.
99. *Ibid.*, 227-235.
100. *Lee*, IV, p. 122. Freeman did not state any time when the conversation took place, but he described it as occurring after Lee had talked to Venable, which, according to his time schedule, was "about 8 o'clock.
101. Alexander, "Lee at Appomattox," 925.
102. MS Copy of Alexander, E. P., *Military Memoirs of a Confederate.* Southern Historical Collection, University of North Carolina Library, Chapel Hill, North Carolina.
103. *Lee*, IV, p. 119.
104. *Lee*, IV, p. 122. Morris Schaff has the same error in *The Sunset of the Confederacy.* 231.
105. *Ibid.*, 603.
106. MS Copy of Alexander, E. P., *Military Memoirs of a Confederate.* Southern Historical Collection, University of North Carolina Library, Chapel Hill, North Carolina.
107. Alexander, E. P., "General Lee at Appomattox," *The Southern Magazine, XII* (1873), 747-752.
108. Alexander E. P., "Lee at Appomattox," *The Century Illustrated Monthly Magazine,* LXIII (1902), 921-931.
109. Alexander, "Lee at Appomattox," 927.
110. *Ibid.*, 927.
111. Longstreet, *op. cit.*, 625.
112. Taylor, W. H., *Four Years with General Lee,* 151-152.
113. Alexander, *Military Memoirs,* 606.
114. Taylor, W. H., *General Lee, His Campaigns in Virginia 1861-1865, with Personal Reminiscences.* Norfolk: Nusbaum and News Co., 1906, p. 288.
115. Maurice, *op. cit.*, 263.
116. Humphreys, *op. cit.*, 392.
117. Maurice, *op. cit.*, 263-264.
118. *O. R.*, XLVI, Pt. 3, p. 664.
119. *Lee*, IV, pp. 124-125.
120. Humphreys, *op. cit.*, 392.
121. Alexander, "Lee at Appomattox," 927.
122. Humphreys, *op. cit.*, 393-394.
123. Maurice, *op. cit.*, 264-265.
124. Longstreet, *op. cit.*, 626-627.
125. Maurice, *op. cit.*, 266.
126. *Ibid.*, 266.
127. *Lee*, IV, p. 129, Also see pp. 513-514.
128. *O. R.*, XLVI, Pt. 3, pp. 667-668.
129. *O. R.*, XLVI, Pt. 1, p. 605.
130. *O. R.*, XLVI, Pt. 3, p. 665.
131. Porter, Horace, "The Surrender at Appomattox Court House," *Battles and Leaders.* Vol. IV, p. 733.
132. *O. R.* XLVI, Pt. 3, p. 664; Dowdey and Manarin, *op. cit.*, 933.
133. *Lee*, IV, p. 128.
134. *O. R.*, XLVI, Pt. 1, p. 605.
135. Thomas, *op. cit.*, 321-323.
136. *O. R.*, XLVI, Pt. 3, p. 665.
137. Grant, *op. cit.*, 339.
138. *Lee*, IV, p. 132.
139. Cullum, G. W. *Biographical Register of the Officers and Graduates of the United States Military Academy, West Point, New York.* Vol. II. New York and Boston: Houghton, Mifflin and Co., 1881, p. 771.
140. Grant, *op. cit.*, 341.
141. *Lee*, IV, p. 129.
142. Alexander, "Lee at Appomattox," 929.
143. Hallam, J. W., "Lee's Surrender," The Philadelphia *Weekly Times,* June 23, 1877.
144. MS Copy of *Military Memoirs of a Confederate.* Southern Historical Collection, University of North Carolina, Chapel Hill, North Carolina.
145. Maurice, *op. cit.*, 266.
146. McDonald, W. N., "Lee's Retreat," *The Southern Bivouac,* I (1882-83) 32.
147. Sheridan said that Longstreet handed him the duplicate of the surrender letter when the officers met at the Court House following the suspension of hostilities. Sheridan then sent it to Grant by Colonel Newhall. Sheridan, *op. cit.*, 198.
148. Talcott, T. M. R., "Retreat from Petersburg to Appomattox C. H.," *S. H. S. P.* XXXII (1904), 72
149. Taylor, *General Lee,* 289-290.
150. Schaff, *op. cit.*, 245. Schaff was mistaken in saying that Colonel John Fairfax accompanied Forsyth. Lee sent Colonel Walter H. Taylor on this mission. Taylor, *General Lee,* 289-290.

151. *O. R.,* XLVI, Pt. 3, p. 666.
152. Longstreet, *op cit.,* 627-628.
153. *Lee,* IV, p. 131.
154. Alexander, "Lee at Appomattox," 930.
155. *Lee,* IV, p. 131.
156. Hallam, *op. cit.*
157. Taylor, *General Lee,* 290.
158. Porter, *op. cit.,* 735.
159. Maurice, *op. cit.,* 267.
160. Taylor, *op. cit.,* 290.
161. Thomas, *op. cit.,* 324.
162. Porter, *op. cit.,* 735.
163. *O. R.,* XLVI, Pt. 1, p. 605.
164. Badeau, Adam, *Military History of Ulysses S. Grant, From April, 1861 to April, 1865.* Vol. III. New York: D. Appleton and Co., 1885, p. 607.
165. Longstreet, *op. cit.,* 626-627.
166. Smith, *op. cit.,* 590; Schaff, *op. cit.,* 241.
167. Smith, *op. cit.,* 591.
168. Gordon, *op. cit.,* 438-439.
169. *Ibid.,* 441.
170. Blackford, C. M., ed., *Memoirs of Life In and Out of the Army in Virginia during the War Between the States.* Vol. II. Lynchburg: J. P. Bell, ca. 1896, Appendix I, p. II.
171. Smith, *op. cit.,* 591.
172. Blackford, *op. cit.,* page I.
173. Sheridan, *op. cit.,* 194-196.
174. Chamberlain, J. L., *The Passing of the Armies.* New York: G. P. Putnam's Sons, 1915, p. 240.
175. *Ibid.,* 241, note 1.
176. McKenna, C. F., ed., *Under the Maltese Cross.* Pittsburg; The 155th Regimental Association, 1910, p. 686.
177. *Ibid.,* 680.
178. *Ibid.,* 686.
179. *Ibid.,* 693-694.
180. Chamberlain, *The Passing of the Armies,* 241. and note 1.
181. *Ibid.,* 241.
182. *Ibid.,* 242, note 1.
183. *Ibid.,* 244.
184. *O. R.,* XLVI, Pt. 1, p. 878.
185. *Ibid.,* 878.
186. *Ibid.,* 1156.
187. Statement of M. J. Billmyer in unidentified newspaper clipping in Munford-Ellis Papers, Duke University, Durham, North Carolina.
188. Smith, *op. cit.,* 590.
189. Alexander, "Lee at Appomattox," 929.
190. The Newberry (S. C.) *Herald,* Extra Edition. April 20, 1865; Moore, E. A., *The Story of a Cannoneer Under Stonewall Jackson.* Lynchburg: J. P. Bell Co., 1910, p. 303.
191. Merington, M., *The Custer Story.* New York: Devin-Adair Co., 1950, p. 157.
192. *Ibid.,* 156.
193. Monaghan, Jay, *Custer.* Boston: Little, Brown and Co., 1959, p. 244.
194. Smith, *op. cit.,* 591.
195. LaBree, Ben., ed., *Camp Fires of the Confederacy.* Louisville: Courier-Journal Co., 1898, pp. 461-462.
196. Smith, *op. cit.,* 591.
197. Schaff, *op. cit.,* 241; Davis, Burke, *To Appomattox.* New York: Popular Library, 1960, p. 332.
198. Freeman, D. S., *Lee's Lieutenants.* Vol. III. New York: Charles Scribner's Sons, 1944. pp. 733-734.
199. Colston, F. M., "Recollections of the Last Months in the Army of Northern Virginia," *S. H. S. P.,* XXXVIII (1910), 11-12.
200. Smith, *op. cit.,* 591.
201. *Lee's Lieutenants,* III, pp. 735-736, note 33.
202. MS Narrative by "An Officer" of the 2nd Virginia Cavalry. *Munford Ellis Papers,* Duke University, Durham, North Carolina.
203. MS Narrative of Lee's Retreat by E. K. Talbot; MS Letter from Charles Talbot to A. C. Young, in *Ellis-Munford Papers,* University of Virginia Library, Charlottesville, Virginia.
MS Letter from S.B.M. Young to T. T. Munford, June 19, 1905, *Munford-Ellis Papers,* Duke University Library, Durham, North Carolina.
204. Young, *op. cit.* Young did not mention Crook as being present at this conference.

205. *O. R.*, XLVI, Pt. 1, p. 1156.
206. *O. R.*, XLVI, Pt. 3, pp. 813-814.
207. *Ibid.*, 882.
208. *Ibid.*, 881.
209. Statement by M. J. Billmyer in unidentified newspaper clipping in Munford-Ellis Papers, Duke University, Durham, North Carolina.
210. *Lee's Lieutenants*, Vol. III. New York: Charles Scribner's Sons, 1944, pp. 667, 852.
211. Warner, E. J., *Generals in Gray*, Baton Rouge: Louisiana State University Press, 1959, Introduction, p. xix.
212. Gibbon, John, "Personal Recollections of Appomattox," *The Century Illustrated Monthly Magazine*, LXIII, (1902), 939.
213. MS Report of C. M. Wilcox. Lee Headquarters Papers. Virginia Historical Society, Richmond, Virginia.
214. *O. R.*, XLVI, Pt. 1, p. 1162.
215. Merritt, Wesley, "Notes on the Surrender of Lee," *The Century Illustrated Monthly Magazine*, LXIII (1902), 944.
216. Blakeman, A. N., ed., *Personal Recollections of the War of the Rebellion.* Third Series. New York: G. P. Putnam's Sons, 1907, pp. 269-270.
217. Schaff, *op. cit.*, 245.
218. Hamilton, M. W., "Augustus C. Buell, Fraudulent Historian," *The Pennsylvania Magazine of History and Biography*, LXXX (1956), 478-492.
219. Buell, Augustus, *The Cannoneer.* Washington: The National Tribune, 1890, p. 375.
220. Badeau, Adam, *Military History of Ulysses S. Grant, From April, 1861 to April, 1865.* Vol. III. New York: D. Appleton and Co., 1885, pp. 597-598.
221. *Map of Appomattox Court House and Vicinity.* Published by Henderson and Co., 1866. Printed *in Appomattox Court House National Historical Park*, 5. Published by the National Park Service.
222. Taylor, W. H., *Four Years with General Lee.* New York: D. Appleton and Co., 1877, pp. 152-153.
223. Pendleton, W. N., "Personal Recollections of General Lee," *The Southern Magazine*, XV (1874), 634.
224. Maurice, *op. cit.*, 268.
225. Probably because he was following Horace Porter's account, Freeman failed to mention Babcock's orderly. *Lee*, IV, p. 133. Marshall definitely mentioned Babcock's orderly as being in the group. Maurice, *op. cit.*, 268. Cadwallader said that Babcock's orderly was Lieutenant *W. M. Dunn.* Thomas, *op. cit.*, 323.
226. Schaff, Morris, *The Spirit of Old West Point, 1858-1862.* Boston and New York: Houghton, Mifflin and Co., 1908, p. 170.
227. *Ibid.*, 170.
228. Maurice, *op. cit.*, 268.
229. *Lee*, IV, p. 134.
230. Maurice, *op. cit.*, 268.
231. Although it is generally stated that Babcock wrote nothing about Appomattox, a check was made at several likely places in the hope that some item might have been overlooked. The only thing uncovered was a letter in the Babcock Collection, Rochester Historical Society, Rochester, New York, in which Babcock merely mentions that he was present at Appomattox Court House.
232. *Op. cit.*, 771.
233. *1884 Annual Reunion of the Association of Graduates, West Point, New York.* East Saginaw, Michigan: E. W. Lyon, Publisher, 1884, p. 127.
234. Porter, *op. cit.*, 735.
235. Maurice, *op. cit.*, 269.
236. *Lee*, p. 135, and note 73.
237. Schaff, Morris, *The Sunset of the Confederacy.* Boston: John W. Luce and Co., 1912, p. 253.
238. Maurice, *op. cit.*, 268.
239. Schaff, *op. cit.*, 263.
240. Sheridan, P. H., *Personal Memoirs of P. H. Sheridan*, Vol. II. New York: Charles L. Webster and Co., 1888, p. 200.
241. Porter, *op. cit.*, 735.
242. *Ibid.*, 735.
243. *Lee*, IV, p. 135.
244. Grant, *op. cit.*, 341.
245. Maurice, *op. cit.*, 269.
246. Sheridan, *op. cit.*, 201.
247. Porter, *op. cit.*, 737.
248. *Lee*, IV, p. 135.
249. Grant, *op. cit.*, 342.
250. Maurice, *op. cit.*, 269.
251. *Ibid.*, 266.
252. Porter, *op. cit.*, 737.
253. *Lee*, IV, p. 135.
254. Sheridan, *op. cit.*, 201.
255. Grant, *op. cit.*, 342.

256. *Ibid.*, 343.
257. *Lee,* IV, p. 139.
258. Marshall, "The Last Days of Lee's Army," 934.
259. Grant, *op. cit.*, 342.
260. Maurice, *op. cit.*, 269-270.
261. *Ibid.*, 270.
262. Grant, *op. cit.*, 343.
263. Jones, J. W., *Personal Reminiscences, Anecdotes, and Letters of General Robert E. Lee.* New York: D. Appleton and Co., 1875, p. 304.
264. Badeau, *op. cit.*, 608.
265. *Lee,* IV, p. 137.
266. Parker, A. C., *The Life of General Ely S. Parker.* Buffalo: The Buffalo Historical Society, 1919, pp. 135-137.
267. Meridith, Roy, *The Face of Robert E. Lee in Life and in Legend.* New York: Charles Scribner's Sons, 1947, p. 127.
268. Parker, *op. cit.*, 130.
269. Grant, *op. cit.*, 344.
270. Porter, *op. cit.*, 738.
271. *Lee,* IV, 142, note 89.
272. Grant, *op. cit.*, 346.
273. Parker, *op. cit.*, 130.
274. *Lee,* IV, p. 137.
275. Grant, *op. cit.*, 341-342.
276. *O. R.*, XLVI, Pt. 3, p. 666.
277. Porter, *op. cit.*, 739.
278. Grant, *op. cit.*, 344.
279. *Ibid.*, 344-345.
280. *Ibid.*, 345.
281. Porter, *op. cit.*, 740.
282. Parker, *op. cit.*, 131.
283. Maurice, *op. cit.*, 371.
284. *Ibid.*, 272.
285. *Ibid.*, 271.
286. Sharpe, G. H., "At Appomattox," The Philadelphia *Weekly Times,* June 30, 1877.
287. Porter, *op. cit.*, 741-742.
288. Porter, *op. cit.*, 741.
289. Grant, *op. cit.*, 346.
290. *Lee,* IV, p. 141. note 82.
291. Porter, *op. cit.*, 741.
292. *O. R.*, XLVI, Pt. 1, p. 1282.
293. "The Dawn of Peace," The Washington (D.C.) *Evening Star,* April 5, 1890.
294. *Op. cit.*, 741.
295. Parker, *op. cit.*, 133.
296. Sharpe, *op. cit.*
297. Porter, *op. cit.*, 741.
298. Parker, *op. cit.*, 133.
299. Sheridan, *op. cit.*, 201-202.
300. Maurice, *op. cit.*, 269.
301. Sheridan, *op. cit.*, 201.
302. Grant, *op. cit.*, 346.
303. Porter, *op. cit.*, 741.
304. Sheridan, *op. cit.*, p. 201.
305. Grant, *op. cit.*, 341.
306. Forsyth, G. A., "The Closing Scene at Appomattox Court House," *Harper's New Monthly Magazine,* XCVI (1897-1898), 707-708.
307. Merritt, Wesley, "Note on the Surrender of Lee," *The Century Illustrated Monthly Magazine,* LXIII (1902), 944.
308. Sharpe, *op. cit.*
309. Forsyth, *op. cit.*, 708.
310. Porter, *op. cit.*, 704.
311. Schaff, *The Spirit of Old West Point,* 170
312. Thomas, *op. cit.*, 326.
313. Maurice, *op. cit.*, 272.

314. *O. R.,* XLVI, Pt. 3, p. 666.
315. Maurice, *op. cit.,* 273.
316. Grant, *op. cit.,* 346-347.
317. Marshall, Charles, "The Last Days of Lee's Army," *The Century Illustrated Monthly Magazine,* LXIII (1902), 935.
318. Porter, *op. cit.,* 742.
319. *Lee,* IV, p. 142, note 88.
320. Grant, *op. cit.,* 342.
321. Porter, *op. cit.,* 737.
322. Sharpe, *op. cit.*
323. "Tributes to General Lee," *The Southern Magazine,* X (1871), 43.
324. Badeau, *op. cit.,* 607.
325. *O. R.,* XLVI, Pt. 3, p. 668.
326. Porter, *op. cit.,* 741.
327. *O. R.,* XLVI, Pt. 3, p. 695. They were sent to Annapolis, Maryland, under charge of their officers, to be released. *Ibid.,* 711.
328. *Lee,* IV, p. 142.
329. Porter, *op. cit.,* 742.
330. Maurice, *op. cit.,* 273.
331. Schaff, *op. cit.,* 275.
332. Sheridan, *op. cit.,* 202.
333. Alexander, E. P., "General Lee at Appomattox," *The Southern Magazine,* XII (1873), 752.
334. Alexander, "Lee at Appomattox," 930.
335. *O. R.,* XLVI, Pt. 1, p. 605.
336. *O. R.,* XLVI, Pt. 1, p. 1178.
337. Porter, *op. cit.,* 743.
338. *Lee,* IV, p. 143.
339. Forsyth, *op. cit.,* 710.
340. *O. R.,* XLVI, Pt. 3, p. 668; Parker, *op. cit., 135.*
341. Morrison, J. L., Jr., *The Memoirs of Henry Heth.* M. A. Thesis at the University of Virginia, 1960, pp. 308-309.
342. Sharpe, *op. cit.*
343. Smith, *op. cit.,* 593.
344. Alexander, E. P., "General Lee At Appomattox," *The Southern Magazine,* XII (1873), 752.
345. MS Copy *Military Memoirs of a Confederate.* Southern Historical Collection, University of North Carolina Library, Chapel Hill, N.C.
346. Colston, F. M., "Recollections of the Last Months in the Army of Northern Virginia," *S. H. S. P.,* XXXVIII (1910), 12.
347. Maurice, Sir Frederick, *Robert E. Lee The Soldier.* Boston and New York: Houghton, Mifflin Co., 1925, p. 292.
348. Alexander, "Lee at Appomattox," 930.
349. Lawley, Francis, "The Last Six Days of Secessia," *The Fortnightly Review,* II (1865), 9-10.
350. Alexander, "General Lee at Appomattox," 752.
351. MS Copy of *Military Memoirs of a Confederate.* Southern Historical Collection, University of North Carolina, Chapel Hill, N.C.
352. Blackford, *op. cit.,* IV.
353. *Ibid.,* V-VI.
354. Badeau, *op. cit.,* 608.
355. Plum, W. R., *The Military Telegraph During the Civil War in the United States.* Vol. II. Chicago: Jansen, McClurg and Co., 1882, p. 326.
356. *O. R.,* XLVI, Pt. 3, p. 683.
357. *O. R.,* XLVI, Pt. 3, pp. 663-664.
358. *Ibid.,* 683.
359. Stern, Philip Van Doren, An End to Valor. Boston: The Houghton Mifflin Co., 1958, p. 298.
360. Mackay, W. K., "Philadelphia During the Civil War." *The Pennsylvania Magazine of History and Biography,* LXX (1946), 45
361. Porter, *op. cit.,* 744.
362. Ross, Ishbel, *The General's Wife.* New York: Dodd, Mead and Co., 1959, p. 187.
363. Morrison, J. L., Jr., *The Memoirs of Henry Heth.* M. A. Thesis, University of Virginia, 1960, pp. 306-307.
364. *O. R.,* XLVI, Pt. 3, p. 710.
365. *O. R.,* XLVI, Pt. 3, p. 666.
366. *O. R.,* XLVI, Pt. 3, pp. 666-667.
367. Parker, *op. cit.,* 134.
368. Maurice, *op. cit.,* 274. Freeman seemed to think that the evidence on this point was inconclusive. He said that the commissioners were appointed by Lee on the day of the surrender but "it is not known where or at what hour." *Op. cit.,* 146.
369. *O. R.,* XLVI, Pt. 3, pp. 685-686.

370. Gibbon, *op. cit.,* 941.
371. *Ibid.,* 943.
372. Blakeman, A. N., ed., *Personal Recollections of the War of the Rebellion.* Third Series. New York: G. P. Putnam's Sons, 1907, p. 273.
373. *O. R.,* XLVI, Pt. 3, p. 685.
374. *O. R.,* XLVI, Pt. 3, p. 685.
375. Grant, *op. cit.,* 347-348.
376. Maurice, *op. cit.,* 278.
377. Thomas, *op. cit.,* 334.
378. Badeau, op. cit., 610.
379. Parker, A. C., *The Life of General Ely S. Parker.* Buffalo: The Buffalo Historical Society, 1919, p. 139.
380. *Lee,* IV, p. 149.
381. *Op. cit.,* 137.
382. *Op. cit.,* 609.
383. *Op. cit.,* 745.
384. Thomas, *op. cit.,* 334.
385. *Lee,* IV, pp. 149-150.
386. Sylvanus Cadwallader's statement that Lee made an appointment to meet Grant on April 10 at 10 A.M. before they left the McLean House on the afternoon of April 9 cannot be regarded as trustworthy. See Thomas, *op. cit.,* 328. This does not agree with Grant's account.
387. Porter, *op. cit.,* 745.
388. *Lee,* IV, p. 150.
389. Thomas, *op. cit.,* 334.
390. Gibson, J. T., Typewritten Letter to Gen. J. A. Early in the *Jubal A. Early Papers,* Jones Memorial Library, Lynchburg, Va.
391. Grant, *op. cit.,* 348.
392. Thomas, *op. cit.,* 334. Grant evidently told C. A. Dana, the Assistant Secretary of War, that Lee made such a statement to him. *O. R., XLVI, Pt. 3, p. 716.*
393. *O. R.,* XLVI, Pt. 3, p. 716.
394. *Lee,* IV, p. 151, note 5.
395. Maurice, *op. cit.,* 275.
396. Porter, *op. cit.,* 746.
397. Maurice, *op. cit.,* 274.
398. Badeau, *op. cit.,* 611. These three are the ones mentioned by Freeman. *Lee,* IV, p. 151.
399. Gibbon, *op. cit.,* 940.
400. *Ibid.,* 942.
401. *Ibid.,* 940-941.
402. *Ibid.,* 941.
403. *O. R.,* XLVI, Pt. 3, p. 693.
404. Parker, *op. cit.,* 139-140.
405. Parker, *op. cit.,* 139-140; O. R., XLVI, Pt. 3, p. 687.
406. *O. R.,* XLVI, Pt. 3, p. 1392; The Newberry (S.C.) *Herald,* Extra Edition, April 20, 1865.
407. *O. R.,* XLVI, Pt. 3, p. 686.
408. Porter, *op. cit.,* 745.
409. *Lee,* IV, p. 150. Although Freeman did not cite Porter at this point, much of his language is similar to that used by Porter and must have come from Porter.
410. Badeau, *op. cit.,* 610.
411. *O. R.,* XLVI, Pt. 3, p. 716.
412. Parker, *op. cit.,* 138-139.
413. Grant, *op. cit.,* 348-349.
414. *Lee,* IV, pp. 520-521.
415. Agassiz, G. R., ed., *Meade's Headquarters 1863-1865.* Boston: Massachusetts Historical Society, 1922, p. 359.
416. Colston, F. M., "Recollections of the Last Months in the Army of Northern Virginia," *S. H. S. P.,* XXXVIII (1910), 13.
417. Fields, J. E., "Robert E. Lee's Farewell Order," *The Autograph Collector's Journal,* I (January 1949), 4.
418. Marshall, Charles, "General Lee's Farewell Address to His Army," *Battles and Leaders,* Volume IV, p. 747.
419. Colston, F. M., "Recollections of the Last Months in the Army of Northern Virginia," *S. H. S. P.,* XXXVIII (1910), 13.
420. Marshall, "General Lee's Farewell Address," 747.
421. "Norforkian Penned Lee's Order for Surrender At Appomattox," Norfolk *Virginian-Pilot,* May 21, 1951.
422. Marshall, "General Lee's Farewell Address," 747.
423. *Lee,* IV, p. 154.

424. *Ibid.*, 154
425. Fields, *op. cit.*, 5.
426. *Lee,* IV, pp. 154-155.
427. Schaff, *op. cit.*, 293-294.
428. *O. R.*, XLVI, Pt. 1, p. 1267.
429. *O. R.*, XLVI, Pt. 3, p. 744.
430. Marshall, "General Lee's Farewell Address," 747.
431. "Norfolkian Penned Lee's Order for Surrender at Appomattox," Norfolk *Virginian-Pilot,* May 21, 1951.
432. The Newberry (S. C.) *Herald,* Extra Edition, April 20, 1865.
433. Fields, *op. cit.*, 5.
434. Dowdey, Clifford and Manarin, L. H., eds. *The Wartime Papers of R. E. Lee.* Boston: Little, Brown and Co., 1961, pp. 934-935. The text in this book has a misprint: "the result" should be "this result".
435. Fields, *op. cit.*, 19.
436. Schaff, *The Sunset of the Confederacy,* 301.
437. Jones, V. C., Gray Ghosts and Rebel Raiders. New York: Henry Holt and Co., 1956, p. 415.
438. Unpublished MS Diary of Eugene Henry Levy in American Jewish Archives, Cincinnati 20, Ohio. Notation on back of photostat copy: "Please Credit the Archives."
439. Forsyth, *op. cit.*, 711.
440. Eliot, Ellsworth, Jr., *West Point in the Confederacy.* New York: G. A. Baker and Co., 1941, p. 78.
441. *Op. Cit.*, 941. In *O. R.*, XLVI, Pt. 3, pp. 709-710, the parole passes are called printed certificates.
442. *Lee's Lieutenants,* III, p. 744.
443. Wellman, M. W., *Rebel Boast.* New York: Henry Holt and Co., 1956, above illustration of parole pass facing page 97.
444. *O. R.*, XLVI, Pt. 3, pp. 709-710.
445. The Newberry (S. C.) *Herald,* Extra Edition, April 20, 1865. It was said in this newspaper that this parole of honor was signed by Fitzhugh Lee. This form does not appear in *O. R.*
446. Gibbon, *op. cit.*, 942.
447. Text in *O. R.*, XLVI, Pt. 3, p. 667. Facsimile in *Lee,* IV. Facing page 150. Photostat copy at A C H N H P.
448. *O. R.*, XLVI, Pt. 1, pp. 57-58.
449. *O. R.*, XLVI, Pt. 3, p. 666.
450. Cockrell, M. F., ed., *Gunner with Stonewall.* Jackson, Tennessee: McCowat-Mercer Press, 1957, p. 128.
451. *O. R.*, XLVI, Pt. 3, P. 706; Blakeman, *Op. cit.*, 274.
452. *Lee's Lieutenants,* III, p. 744.
453. Cockrell, *op. cit.*, 128-129.
454. McCarthy, Carlton, *Soldier Life in the Army of Northern Virginia 1861-1865.* Richmond: B. F. Johnson Publishing Co., 1908, pp. 163164.
455. "The Opposing Forces in the Appomattox Campaign." *Battles and Leaders,* IV, p. 753.
456. *Ibid.*, 753.
457. *O. R.*, XLVI, Pt. 3, p. 696.
458. Diary of Eugene Henry Levy, a member of Dreux's (Louisiana) Battery, in Marcus, R. M., and Ochs, A. S., eds., *Memoirs of American Jews 1775-1865.* Vol. III. Philadelphia: The Jewish Publication Society of America, 1956, pp. 315-316.
459. *O. R.*, XLVI, Pt. 3, p. 706.
460. Chamberlain, J. L., "The Last Salute of the Army of Northern Virginia," *S. H. S. P.*, XXXII (1904), 360. Chamberlain definitely stated that the day was "the 10th of April, in 1865." *Ibid.*, 360. Pullen was mistaken in thinking that it was April 9. *Op. cit.*, 269.
461. *Lee's Lieutenants,* III, pp. 744-745.
462. Blakeman, *op. cit.*, 273.
463. Chamberlain, *Passing of the Armies,* 255, 257.
464. Chamberlain, "The Last Salute," 360.
465. Blakeman, *op. cit.*, 273.
466. *Ibid.*, 273.
467. Smith, *Antietam to Appomattox,* 594.
468. *Lee's Lieutenants,* III, p. 746, note 82.
469. Pullen, J. J., *The Twentieth Maine.* Philadelphia: J. B. Lippincott, 1957, p. 271.
470. Chamberlain, "Last Salute," 361; Pullen included the 62nd Pennsylvania among the troops in the Union line. *Op. cit.*, 271. The 62nd was not included in the troops listed in the *Official Records,* XLVI, Pt. 1.
471. Chamberlain, "Last Salute," 361.
472. Pullen, *op. cit.*, 272.
473. *Ibid.*, 272.
474. Blakeman, *op. cit.*, 275.
475. *Ibid.*, 275.
476. Pullen, *op. cit.*, 268.

477. Blakeman, *op. cit.,* 276.
478. *Lee's Lieutenants,* III, p. 747, note 87.
479. Chamberlain, "Last Salute," 362.
480. Blakeman, *op. cit.,* 278.
481. *Ibid.,* 275-278.
482. Chamberlain, "Last Salute," 362.
483. Blakeman, *op. cit.,* 275.
484. Smith, *op. cit.,* 595.
485. *Ibid.,* 595-596.
486. Chamberlain, "Last Salute," 361.
487. Smith, *op. cit.,* 596. Chamberlain reported that he collected 400 or 500 stand of arms and stacked them near the road. He said that there were also remaining in the camp 1 light 12-pounder brass piece of artillery, some 20 caissons, and a large number of uninjured wagons. *O. R.,* XLVI, Pt. 3, p. 731.
488. "The Opposing Forces in the Appomattox Campaign." *Battles and Leaders,* IV, p. 753. Names taken from the parole lists were published in Volume XV, *Southern Historical Society Papers.*
489. *O. R.,* XLVI, Pt. 1, p. 1265.
490. *O. R.,* XLVI, Pt. 3, p. 734.
491. Alexander, "Lee at Appomattox," 931.
492. Claiborne, J. H., "Last Days of Lee and His Paladins," 51.
493. Unpublished Manuscript Diary of Eugene Henry Levy, American Jewish Archives, Cincinnati 20, Ohio. Notation on back of photostat copy. "Please credit the Archives."
494. *O. R.,* XLVI, Pt. 3, p. 1395.
495. Gibbon, "Personal Recollections of Appomattox," 942-943.
496. Lee, G. T., "Reminiscences of General Robert E. Lee, 1865-68," *The South Atlantic Quarterly,* XXVI, (1927), 239.
497. *O. R.,* XLVI, Pt. 3, p. 749.
498. McDonald, W. N. "Lee's Retreat," *The Southern Bivouac,* I (1882-1883), 32.
499. Blackford, *op. cit.,* p. II.
500. Hagood, James R., *Memoirs of the First South Carolina Regiment of Volunteer Infantry in the Confederate War for Independence from April 12, 1861 to April 10, 1865,* p. 215. Typescript. South Carolinia Library, University of South Carolina, Columbia, S. C.
501. Cockrell, M. F., ed., *Gunner With Stonewall.* Jackson, Tennessee: McCowat-Mercer Press, 1957, p. 125.
502. McCarthy, *op. cit.,* 161.
503. Macon, T. J., *Reminiscences of the First Company of Richmond Howitzers.* Richmond: Whittet and Shepperson, (N.D.), 44-45.
504. Moore, E. A., *The Story of a Cannoneer Under Stonewall Jackson.* Lynchburg: J. P. Bell Co., 1910, p. 305.
505. McCarthy, *op. cit.,* 159.
506. Alexander, "Lee at Appomattox," 931.
507. Pullen, *op. cit.,* 267.
508. Blakeman, A. N., *op. cit.,* 269.
509. Blakeman, A. N., ed., *op. cit.,* 238.
510. "March of the Army of the James," The New York Freeman's Journal and Catholic Register, April 22, 1865.
511. Unidentified Newspaper Clipping in H. B. *McClelland Papers,* Virginia Historical Society, Richmond, Virginia.
512. Stewart, *op. cit.,* 270.
513. Gibbon, "Personal Recollections of Appomattox," 940.
514. *Ibid.,* 940.
515. Grant, *op. cit.,* 347.
516. Stewart, *op. cit.,* 269.
517. *Ibid.,* 270-271.
518. Alexander, "Lee at Appomattox," 930.
519. Moore, E. A., *The Story of a Cannoneer Under Stonewall Jackson.* Lynchburg: J. P. Bell Co., 1910, pp. 304-305.
520. Chamberlain, *The Passing of the Armies,* 257.
521. *O. R.,* XLVI, Pt. 3, p. 710.
522. *Ibid.,* 695.
523. Munford, G. W., to his wife, April 21, 1865. MS Letter in *Munford-Ellis Papers,* Duke University Durham, N.C.
524. *O. R.,* XLVI, Pt. 3, p. 716.
525. *Ibid.,* 763.
526. Alexander, "Lee at Appomattox," 930.
527. Coffin, C. C., *Four Years of Fighting: A Volume of Personal Observation with the Army and Navy, from the First Battle of Bull Run to the Fall of Richmond.* Boston: Ticknor and Fields, 1866, p. 554.
528. *Ibid.,* 553.
529. Pickett, L. C., *Pickett and His Men.* Atlanta: The Foote and Davies Co., 1899, p. 393.

530. *Lee,* IV, p. 155.
531. *O. R.,* XLVI, Pt. 1, p. 1282.
532. Rosser, T. L., "Appomattox," The Philadelphia *Weekly Times,* April 5, 1885.
533. Chamberlain, J. L., *The Passing of the Armies.* New York: G. P. Putnam's Sons, 1915, pp. 265-266.
534. *O. R.,* XLVI, Pt. 1, pp. 1266-1267.
535. Dowdey and Manarin, *op. cit.,* 938-939.
536. Taylor, *Four Years With General Lee,* 156.
537. *O. R.,* XLVI, Pt. 1, p. 895.
538. *Ibid.,* 908.
539. *O. R.,* XLVI, Pt. 1, p. 605.
540. Sheridan, *op. cit.,* 204.
541. *Ibid.,* 202.
542. *O. R.,* XLVI, Pt. 1, p. 1121.
543. *Ibid.,* 1175.
544. *Ibid.,* 1181.
545. *Ibid.,* 60.
546. *O. R.,* XLVI, Pt. 3, pp. 668, 673, 674, 677.
547. Dunn, C. E., "The Fiftieth Anniversary of the Surrender of General Lee," The Aroostook *Pioneer,* April 22, 1915. Quoted in Pullen, J. J., *The Twentieth Maine.* Philadelphia: J. B. Lippincott Co., 1957, p. 270.
548. The Newberry (S. C.) *Herald,* Extra Edition, April 20, 1865.
549. "The Last Ration," *The Southern Bivouac,* I (1885), 217.
550. Pullen, *op. cit.,* 274.
551. McDonald, W. N., "Lee's Retreat," *The Southern Bivouac,* I (1882-83), 33.
552. *O. R.,* XLVI, Pt. 3, p. 668.
553. Thomas, *op. cit.,* 329.
554. Monaghan, J., *op. cit.,* 246.
555. *Ibid.,* 246.
556. Merington, *op. cit.,* 159.
557. Porter, *op. cit.,* 744.
558. Thomas, *op. cit.,* 329.
559. Thomas, *op. cit., 330.*
560. Porter, *Campaigning With Grant,* 487. These details were not given in Porter's account published in *Battles and Leaders.*
561. Thomas, *op. cit.,* 330.
562. Gibbon, *op. cit.,* 941.
563. Alexander was mistaken in thinking that only Confederates were interested in carrying off pieces of the apple tree. Union officers are reported to have offered five and ten dollars for a chip from the apple tree. See Smith, J. L., *Antietam to Appomattox with 118th Penna. Vols., Corn Exchange Regiment.* Philadelphia: J. L. Smith, 1892, pp. 675-676.
564. Alexander, E. P., "Lee at Appomattox," *The Century Illustrated Monthly Magazine,* LXIII (1902), 929-930.
565. Maurice, Frederick, *An Aide-De-Camp of Lee being the Papers of Colonel Charles Marshall.* Boston: Little, Brown, and Co., 1927, p. 267.
566. Hallam, J. W., "Lee's Surrender," The Philadelphia Weekly Times, June 23, 1877. Hallam said that relic hunters carried off "trees, rails and buildings" in the vicinity of the apple tree.
567. Grant, U. S., *Personal Memoirs of U. S. Grant.* Vol. II. New York: The Century Co., 1903, pp. 340-341.
568. Smith, *op. cit.,* 675-676.
569. "Capitulation of Lee's Army," The Newberry (S.C.) *Herald,* Extra Edition, April 20, 1865.
570. Smith, *op. cit.,* 676.
571. Kingsbury, T. B., "Appomattox," *Our Living and Our Dead,* II (1875), 54.
572. Smith, *op. cit.,* 678.
573. Jones, T. G., "The Last Nine Days of the War in Virginia," *The Cycle,* September 2, 1876.
574. Grant, *op. cit.,* 346.
575. Jones, J. W., *Personal Reminiscences, Anecdotes, and Letters of General Robert E. Lee.* New York: D. Appleton and Company, 1875, p. 303.
576. *Lee,* IV, pp. 142-143, note 89.
577. Jones, *op. cit.,* 303-304.
578. "Capitulation of Lee's Army," The Newberry (S.C.) *Herald,* Extra Edition, April 20, 1865.
579. Porter, *op. cit.,* 737.
580. *Ibid.,* 737.
581. Lee, Fitzhugh, *General Lee.* New York: D. Appleton and Co., 1894, p. 394, note.
582. For an account of the presentation of Lee's sword to the Confederate Museum in Richmond see "Sword of Lee Comes Back to Virginia To-Day." The Richmond *Times-Dispatch,* January 30, 1918.
583. Chamberlain, "The Last Salute," 363.

584. *Ibid.*, 934, note 1.
585. Temple, W. C., ed., *Campaigning With Grant.* Bloomington: Indiana University Press, 1961.
586. *Ibid.*, xxii. It should be noted that Porter's narrative is by no means "the only eyewitness account of the Appomattox surrender."
587. *Ibid.*, 525.
588. *Lee,* IV, pp. 141, 142, 151.
589. Porter, *op. cit.*, 735.
590. *Ibid.*, 737.
591. *Ibid.*, 735.
592. *Ibid.*, 735.
593. Maurice, *op. cit.*, 268-269.
594. *Op. cit.*, 735.
595. *Op. cit.*, 268.
596. *Op. cit.*, 735.
597. Sheridan, *op. cit.*, 201.
598. *Op. cit.*, 269.
599. *Op. cit.*, 737.
600. *Op. cit.*, 269.
601. Grant, *op. cit.*, 342.
602. *Op. cit.*, 740.
603. *Op. cit.*, 271.
604. *Op. cit.*, 741.
605. Parker, *op. cit.*, 133.
606. *Op. cit.*, 741.
607. *Ibid.*, XLVI, Pt. 1, p. 1282.
608. *Op. cit.*, 741.
609. Grant, *op. cit.*, 346.
610. *Lee,* IV, p. 141, note 82.
611. *Op. cit.*, 742.
612. *Op. cit.*, 142, note 88.
613. *Op. cit.*, 735, 742.
614. *Op. cit.*, 273.
615. *Op. cit.*, 743.
616. Morrison, J. L., Jr., *The Memoirs of Henry Heth.* M. A. Thesis, University of Virginia, 1960, pp. 308-309.
617. Badeau, *op. cit.*, 608.
618. Parker, *op. cit.*, 135.
619. *Lee,* IV, p. 137.
620. *Op. cit.*, 745.
621. Gibson, J. T., Typewritten Letter to General J. A. Early in the *Jubal A. Early Papers,* Jones Memorial Library, Lynchburg, Virginia.
622. *Op. cit.*, 151, note 5.

INDEX